BRUCHKO

AND THE MOTILONE MIRACLE

BRUCHKO

AND THE MOTILONE MIRACLE

BRUCE OLSON WITH JAMES LUND

Charisma
HOUSE
A STRANG COMPANY

Most Strang Communications/Charisma House/Siloam/FrontLine/Realms products are available at special quantity discounts for bulk purchase for sales promotions, premiums, fund-raising, and educational needs. For details, write Strang Communications/Charisma House/Siloam/FrontLine/Realms, 600 Rinehart Road, Lake Mary, Florida 32746, or telephone (407) 333-0600.

Bruchko and the Motilone Miracle by Bruce Olson with James Lund
Published by Charisma House
A Strang Company
600 Rinehart Road
Lake Mary, Florida 32746
www.charismahouse.com

Scripture quotations are from the King James Version of the Bible, and the Holy Bible, New International Version. Copyright © 1973, 1978, 1984, International Bible Society. Used by permission.

Cover design by studiogearbox.com

Photos courtesy of Bruce Olson and/or Orville and Merry Anderson

Due to issues of government security and religious persecution, some names and details of stories in this book have been changed for the privacy and protection of the persons involved.

Library of Congress Cataloging-in-Publication Data

Olson, Bruce.
  Bruchko and the Motilone miracle / by Bruce Olson ; with James Lund.-- 1st ed.
    p. cm.
  Includes bibliographical references.
  ISBN 1-59185-795-3 (paper back)
  1. Motilon Indians--Missions. 2. Yuko Indians--Missions. 3. Olson, Bruce.
4. Indians of South America--Missions--Venezuela. 5. Missionaries--Venezuela--Biography.
6. Missionaries--United States--Biography. I. Lund, James R. II. Title.
  F2319.2.M6O438 2006
  266.0089'982--dc22

                              2006007725

                    ISBN-13: 978-1-59185-795-2

              06 07 08 09 10 — 9 8 7 6 5 4 3 2
              Printed in the United States of America

To Ashcayra Arabadora Acorora (Jorge Kaymiyokba's son),
Bobby Abrincadura Aberdora (Cobaydrá "Bobby" Bobaríshora's son),
Daniel Adjibacbayra, and Roberto Dacsarara Axdobidora as they strengthen
traditional values and forge the future of the Barì, leading them into the
twenty-first century under the instruction and wisdom of the
tribal elders and the witness of God's Spirit.

Acknowledgments

I wish to thank Merry Anderson for generously making available her collection of my newsletters and other material gathered over a period of more than forty years; Sandra Green, for her assistance in Spanish translation; Jennifer Barrow, for editorial comments; Linda Hohonshelt, for tape transcription; and the entire team at Strang Communications, in particular Stephen Strang, Barbara Dycus, Debbie Marrie, and Dottie McBroom, for their help with this book and for their longtime support of my ministry.

The freshness of Christ's Spirit breathes through the jungles of the Catatumbo. He articulates in the hearts of men and women how peace can reign through the resurrection of His Son.

—Bruce Olson
May 25, 1992

Contents

Note From the Editor

The word *Motilone* comes from the Spanish word *motilar,* meaning "cut hair." Spanish settlers arriving in Venezuela and Colombia in the early 1600s were the first to call the indigenous peoples of the Catatumbo region "Motilones" because of their short hair, but this word does not exist in the tribe's vocabulary. Instead, they call themselves *Barì,* which means "we the people."

In preparing this book for publication, our publishing house wanted to show respect for this ancient people group and not use words that would disparage them in any way. After careful consideration and consultation with people who work in the South American region, we agreed that since the Motilones are accepting of the fact that people call them by their Spanish name, and also of the word *Indian,* we use these terms to identify them in this book.

However, we do make one exception. When the speech of a Motilone is quoted, we use the word *Barì* in all references to their people, since a Motilone would never use any other word to describe himself or his tribe.

Foreword

As I write, I am on an airline flight heading south across Mozambique in east Africa. Below are some of the poorest and most isolated communities on Planet Earth. In the bush they are living as they have lived for centuries, without electricity, running water, or modern communication at all. Most are illiterate, don't use money, and have never seen a teacher, doctor, or policeman. Soon I will be maneuvering a four-wheel-drive truck over rough roads to a remote town where we will hold another of our "bush conferences," preaching Jesus to pagans and animists who have never seen the power of God.

Two weeks after our May wedding twenty-six years ago, my wife, Heidi, and I took off from Los Angeles and headed for Indonesia to begin our missionary lives. We had one-way tickets and thirty dollars in our pockets—and a word from God that we would be in Indonesia, working with Mel Tari, by summer. We have been running the race all these years, fighting the good fight of faith, and enduring trials we never imagined we would face. And during all this time, one testimony has stood out in my heart and memory. The Holy Spirit has used this testimony to encourage me and keep my perspective clean and simple. The testimony is Bruce Olson's incredible story, as told in *Bruchko*.

Bruce Olson was a forerunner for me, a hero of the faith who proved the gospel by his faith and choices, so rare in the Western world. I am a third-generation missionary who grew up listening to my grandfather's stories of revival in old China, but Bruce's stories were recent and taught me just what the Holy Spirit knew I needed to hear again. Bruce was radical, and radically simple. That was the thrill of reading him. The Truth is utterly powerful—if we believe it simply and humbly like a child. The gospel is all true! And the simplest people on Earth can partake of it freely until their lives become monuments to the grace of God.

The Holy Spirit directed my grandfather to take my grandmother to China and lean entirely on Him for support. I also longed to serve God freely, without care, trusting in Him for everything. Could we possibly demonstrate to the poor and suffering that the gospel is sufficient in all circumstances and that we can live the Sermon on the Mount in this world? We don't have to be like unbelievers, always worried about food, clothes, and self-preservation. Bruce Olson simply left, still a very young man, following the leading of the Spirit in his heart, without concern for the usual gauntlet of obstacles to missionary service through traditional channels. I was excited by his example, and my faith mounted.

Bruce's story showed me again just how much love the Holy Spirit is able to plant in a human heart for others, even those very unlikely to capture or command any affection from the outside world. Bruce's whole life is a story of the love of God, pouring out in purity and overcoming power through one person for an entire people group considered for centuries as unreached and unreachable. Today, Heidi and I are reaching out to the four million Makua of Mozambique's northern province of Cabo Delgado, a people group that has also been tagged by missiologists as unreached and unreachable. Bruce's history has helped to keep me on course again and again as today we are bringing in Jesus' Makua bride, whole villages at a time, as He wins their hearts through us as only He can.

I am probably most stirred by Bruce's accounts of how simple hearts in the jungle, unhardened by years of resistance, responded with wide-eyed wonder and sobs of grief and joy at the story of how God Himself came to Earth to die for their sins. What a perfect model of how all of us who call upon the name of Jesus should be thrilled beyond measure by the most fundamental foundations of our salvation. Never should we be tired or bored with what God has done for us or unimpressed with His promises for our future. Never should we become so sophisticated or sidetracked in our spiritual journey that we lose sight of that which sustains all our hope and joy!

Bruce's story has been an ongoing one of progress for the Motilone Indians, a saga of God's total concern for a people's welfare and an instilling of His values in every corner of Motilone society. That the Holy Spirit has held Bruce's hand all these years and kept his heart singularly focused on the welfare of his chosen people is a miraculous record that again helps Heidi and me. From every page of Bruce's book we learn perseverance and attention to goodness, excellence, and detail that are necessary for the long-term guidance of our people in Africa. And Bruce's history with his beloved Motilone people shows that he has shepherded them with a supernaturally imparted sensitivity to their culture, honoring their ways in every way possible in the limitless love of God.

May the heart of every reader of this book be imprinted with the same pure and simple love of God that shaped Bruce's many years in the jungle where he so delighted in a rich taste of the life of heaven itself. And like Bruce, may we all overcome every obstacle to finishing the course set before us so that we may be able to enjoy and glorify our God as we live our lives among the people He has so strongly put on our hearts.

—ROLLAND AND HEIDI BAKER
IRIS MINISTRIES
PEMBA, MOZAMBIQUE

Prologue

It is a beautiful October morning in the equatorial jungle of northeastern Colombia. Slivers of sunrays filter through towering palm trees, striking the abundant green fronds near the jungle floor and sending tendrils of steam skyward. I am walking with fifteen natives of this region, members of the Motilone Indian tribe. In a few minutes we will board a dugout canoe on the bank of the Rio de Oro—the "river of gold"—to travel downriver to Saphadana, the site of a Motilone trading post. I savor each step, relishing the company of the Indians and the tumultuous chorus offered by the exotic birds, monkeys, and katydids that live in the lush greenery around us. I am in no hurry to leave. This is a place of enchantment. Some would even call it paradise.

I have no inkling that in the midst of this paradise a terrible danger hides and waits.

As I climb into the canoe, I glance at Jorge Kaymiyokba, one of the Motilone leaders who has become my close friend over the twenty-six years I've lived and worked among his people. I grin and pull the cord to start the motor as the other Indians squat on the dugout floor. Kaymiyokba returns my grin with a warm smile of his own. We are family, he and I. The Indians crowded around are my brothers and sisters. To an outside observer, I would appear out of place. I am fair-skinned, a lanky six feet three inches, donned in khaki shirt, pants, and sandals; the Indians are brown, stocky, at least half a foot shorter, and wear nothing more than a loincloth or hand-woven canvas skirt. Yet despite our physical differences, I feel truly at home with the Motilones, exactly where I belong on Planet Earth. I am pleased to realize that I am content.

How could I have imagined, when I first walked into the jungle, all that God intended to do here? How was it possible that I had left my family and friends in Minnesota at the age of nineteen to go on a journey that would lead to this exotic place, to these amazing, legendary people—a people so isolated and hostile that no outsider had survived contact with them in four hundred years of recorded history until I walked into their territory?

When I'd boarded the plane to South America in 1961 with nothing but a one-way ticket and a few dollars in my pocket, not knowing one word of Spanish, nearly everyone thought I was foolish—or just plain crazy. But I had been unable to resist the subtle, persistent longing that had drawn me here, the growing love that God had put in my heart for the indigenous tribal people of this continent, the quiet voice inside that told me I would never be happy, never have a moment's peace, until I obeyed His call and demonstrated His love to the Motilones. No, I could not have imagined where that call would take me; I could not have imagined that today my heart and life would be deeply rooted in these people and in this vast, remote jungle.

Nor could I have foreseen the fate that awaited me this day—October 24, 1988—and the consequences it would bring.

It is a good morning for travel. The rainy season is upon us, but the sun is breaking through; the temperature is already over 100 degrees. I am glad for the sun, though it will turn the jungle into a giant steam bath. I've been feeling a malaria attack coming on, and the intense, sweltering heat of our downriver journey just might sweat it out of me—or at least keep my teeth from chattering for a while.

As Kaymiyokba steers the boat, I scan the shorelines on both the Colombian and Venezuelan sides of the river, watching for any guerrillas that might be lurking there. The four major guerrilla organizations in Colombia have operated in the adjacent regions for almost a decade, gradually controlling more and more of the area surrounding traditional Motilone territory. My life has been threatened repeatedly because Colombian revolutionaries see me as the key to controlling the vast Colombia-Venezuela border territory where the Motilones hunt and live. I am only a missionary—but in the eyes of the revolutionaries, I am so influential among the Motilones and neighboring tribes that unless I can be convinced to join their movement and bring the Indians into their cause, they believe the Indians will be a constant threat. Since I have resisted their previous attempts to recruit me, I have been marked for elimination. With me out of the picture, the guerrillas theorize, the Indians will soon yield to their demands. They will then have free rein in northeast Colombia and new territory for establishing training bases for their revolution.

All of this makes me cautious in my journeys through areas such as Saphadana, where the guerrillas seem to be making their presence known with increasing boldness. I am not afraid for myself so much as I am fearful of the bloodshed that could result among the Indians if I am killed. The guerrillas are capable of anything. They have learned to rationalize their kidnappings, executions, bombings, and other crimes by claiming they serve a higher cause: "The people's rebellion."

Now, as we journey downstream, I suddenly feel tense. Yet everyone else seems in good spirits, so I try to relax. After an hour and a half, we approach Saphadana and the Motilone cooperative. I catch a glimpse of the shoreline and immediately notice two guerrillas in camouflage standing in a clearing a short distance from the unoccupied trading post. They carry rifles and machine guns and are watching us intently.

Victor, the Motilone sitting next to me, leans over and whispers, "The guerrillas are looking at us." He exchanges nervous glances with Kaymiyokba.

I avoid glancing in the guerrillas' direction, hoping not to provoke them. We move toward shore until our canoe hits the beach. When Kaymiyokba jumps out to pull the canoe further up onto the sand, I turn my back. Then I step onto the beach. Immediately, a deafening noise splits the air and the sand in front of me bubbles and erupts like a cauldron filled with boiling water.

"Out of the canoe!" a guerrilla shouts. The rest of the Indians disembark. Several of the men march toward the guerrilla pair, obviously intending to attack them with their bare hands. But one of the revolutionaries fires another volley in our direction, which slams into the motor and rips a gaping hole in the side of the canoe.

"Lie down with your faces to the ground!" the same guerrilla orders.

Kaymiyokba continues to walk toward the guerrillas. I can see that he is struggling to control his anger. "Let's discuss this," he says in Spanish. "Let's not start something we'll all regret—"

"There's nothing to discuss!" the guerrilla shouts, spraying the beach with his weapon as punctuation. One of his bullets grazes Kaymiyokba's forehead. The Motilone stands his ground.

"Bruce Olson is taken captive by the UCELN National Liberation Army!" the guerrilla shouts, motioning at me to step toward him. This guerrilla group, commonly known as the ELN, is the only one of the four national revolutionary organizations that has not agreed to an informal truce with the Colombian government after being offered the opportunity to put their agenda before the people in free elections.

I assess our situation, realizing I have only a few seconds to make a decision. There is no way we can successfully resist these men in physical combat; it's likely that there are more armed revolutionaries hiding nearby, and we have no weapons whatsoever, not even bows and arrows. I never carry arms, and on this trip I haven't even brought along a pocketknife—not that it would be any help against machine guns.

Are there other options? I could jump in the river and swim underwater to avoid the guerrillas' bullets and possibly escape downstream. I know the area well, while the guerrillas do not, so my chances would be good. But that would leave the Motilones at their mercy; I cannot risk it. And it would only put off this confrontation to another time, another place.

As the guerrillas train their guns on me, I decide that the moment has come to face the enemy. But I will try to do it on my own terms, in a way that will catch the guerrillas off guard and give the Motilones their best chance to escape unharmed.

I pick up the backpack I'd dropped when the gunfire started and tell Kaymiyokba in Motilone, "Don't follow me. Don't do anything!"

Then I speak to the guerrillas. "I am Olson. I'm the one you want. Leave the Motilones alone."

I turn and begin to walk away from both the guerrillas and the Indians. As I walk, about two dozen more guerrillas emerge from the jungle. I ignore them and keep walking, hoping to put as much distance as I can between them and the Indians. Then someone shouts, "Stop! Stop, or we'll shoot!"

I walk faster and shout over my shoulder, "You came to capture Olson. You can have me, but you'll have to come get me!"

A few guerrillas start after me, walking as quickly as possible without actually running. Finally, when we are about five hundred yards from the Motilones, most of the guerrillas abandon the Indians to chase me.

Suddenly, more revolutionaries appear in front of me. Using their weapons, they knock me to the ground and push my face into the wet earth. They kick me onto my back. One of them roughly shoves the barrel of a rifle into my mouth. I wince as metal scrapes against my teeth.

So this is how I'll die, I think. *From the bullet of a guerrilla's gun.* I am surprised at how calm I am.

But then, I have been prepared to die for a long time. I expected to die more than two decades ago after my first encounter with the Motilones, when I was shot through the thigh with a four-foot arrow, taken to their camp, and held there, expecting to be devoured by cannibals. But God had other purposes in mind for me then, amazing plans that changed my life and the Motilone Indians forever. I have developed an abiding love and respect for these people. There is still so much more for me to share with them, and them with me—but I know that God will take care of the Motilones and complete the work He has started. If God has decided that my time for serving Him with the Motilones is over, who am I to question Him? I have done what I came to the jungle to do. I am at peace, and I will die without regret.

And so I wait for the explosion that will end my life. And in that brief instant, I remember...

—Adapted from an article in *Charisma* magazine,
November 1989, 46–58,
by Bruce Olson as told to Susan DeVore Williams

Chapter 1

Walking on Jesus' Trail

A tall prophet with yellow hair will come to us carrying banana stalks.
Knowledge of life and God will come out of those stalks, and God will
show us the way back to Him.

—ANCIENT MOTILONE LEGEND

I was fourteen years old when I had my first real talk with Jesus. For days I'd
been thinking about Him, repeatedly asking myself, *Who is my God?*

It was a serious question for a young boy to struggle with, but I suppose I was a
rather serious youth. Tall, spindly, and nearsighted, I didn't have a lot of friends.
I was never good at sports. The other kids made fun of me when they threw foot-
ball passes and I couldn't catch them.

I did have one friend, another boy my age named Kent Lange. He came to
my house sometimes on Saturdays, and we would talk about horror stories and
movies we'd seen. We tried to scare each other, and we'd giggle and stick our
heads under the cushions. We enjoyed being scared. But sooner or later we would
talk about God's judgment, about the burning pitch and the sky being rolled up
like a scroll. Then we'd get very quiet. We knew that was no invention of a movie
director or a story writer. It was real.

My father, a stern man and successful investment banker, and my mother had
immigrated to the United States from Norway. Both were traditional Lutherans
who took us to church every Sunday near our home in St. Paul, Minnesota.
That's where I heard the minister announce from the pulpit, "Someday God will
judge and divide everyone. He will separate those who please Him from those
who do not." His sermons frightened me and caused my own heart to condemn
me. I knew that my actions were not always pleasing to God. Perhaps this is what
made me so serious.

On the other hand, life at home was also a grim affair. The four of us—Father,
Mother, my older brother, Dave, and I—just couldn't seem to relate to each other.
It seemed we got along best if we didn't speak to each other at all.

The only time I really felt comfortable and at home was when I was with my
books. I loved to line them up on my bed in a circle around me. I particularly enjoyed

studying Scripture and languages. I'd been reading from the Old Testament for years. More recently I'd begun learning Greek and exploring the New Testament.

But the more Scripture I read, the more confused I became. In the New Testament, Jesus Christ, the Son of God, didn't seem at all like the God of judgment and justice I'd come to fear. Jesus was full of love for others. Everyone who met Him was satisfied and found peace with God.

One night in my room, surrounded by my books, the questions kept swirling in my mind. *Who is my God? Where is He? Does He care about me?* I wanted peace with God.

I decided to read more from the New Testament. I didn't really expect to discover anything helpful. After all, the Bible was written before there were Lutherans. Then I came across a verse that sent electricity surging through my body.

I sat up and read Luke 19:10 again: "For the Son of man is come to seek and to save that which was lost." I knew God's justice, that He would judge me on the basis of my impurities—but here was a verse saying that Jesus has come to save the lost. I knew instantly whom He was talking about: me. But how was Jesus going to save me? And from what?

Hours passed. There didn't seem to be any solution to my questions. I was tired. The clock on my dresser said it was two o'clock in the morning.

Suddenly, I felt a strong urge to try to speak to Christ. Of course I'd prayed before, in church, reading from a hymnal. But this was different.

"Jesus," I began, "I've read about how everyone who encountered You was satisfied. Now I want the same satisfaction. I want peace and fulfillment like Paul and John and James and the other disciples. I want to be delivered from all my fears and—"

At that moment I felt a presence, a stillness, in the room. It was at the same time small and quiet, huge and powerful, covering everything.

"Lord, I'm frightened by You," I continued. "You know I don't even like myself. Everything is messed up around me. And it's messed up *in* me, too. But please, God, I want to be a person who pleases You. I can't do it myself. And I don't understand how You can do anything within me. But Jesus, if You could change all those people in the Bible, I believe You can change me. Please, Jesus, let me know You. Make me new."

Right away, I knew that something *was* changing. I still felt miserable and broken and sick of myself. But I also sensed a peace coming into me. Not something dead or passive. Not just a silence ending the war inside me. It was alive, making *me* alive. And I knew that I didn't ever want that peace, that stillness, to go away.

The peace was still there two years later when I attended my first missionary conference. Mr. Rayburn, a short man in a bright green polka-dot shirt and dirty tennis shoes, spoke about the people in New Guinea who had never even heard of the love of Jesus Christ. It stirred something within me. Unbelievable as it seemed, God was calling me to be a missionary. Because of my fascination with languages, I had dreamed of becoming a linguistics professor. And so, for the next few months, I resisted God's call. But gradually, He began to change my heart. And as my interest in other countries and cultures grew, I found myself drawn to South America and to the native people of two countries in particular: Colombia and Venezuela.

This explains how, in another three years and over my parents' objections, I found myself standing in a small Venezuelan airport, a nineteen-year-old with no friends, no knowledge of the local language, and just seventy dollars in cash. Looking back on it, I can see how people thought I was crazy. Yet from this inauspicious beginning, though I didn't understand it at the time, God kept guiding me to the right next step.

First, He led me to stay at a local boardinghouse for students. A group of young people my own age approached me on the beach the very first morning of my stay in Venezuela. I remember it as if it were yesterday.

Though I had studied several languages during high school and college, I knew only two words in Spanish at that time: "Adios, amigo!" They had an interesting effect on my conversations that first day in Venezuela. When anyone approached me and began talking, I quickly said, "Adios, amigo," and I was left alone!

But as I walked along the beach, I was approached by four university students who were learning English. They were eager to test their skills, so in spite of my limited Spanish, they persisted.

"Where—are—you—going?" they asked in broken English.

"Nowhere," I truthfully replied. I had no plans, no contacts, no support, and no money.

"What—are—you—doing?" came the next carefully rehearsed question.

"Nothing," I answered, assuming that would conclude the conversation.

I knew that something *was* changing.
I sensed a peace coming into me. It was
alive, making *me* alive. And I knew that
I didn't ever want that peace to go away.

To my surprise, they responded, "That's what we're doing! You can do it with us!"

With that, they became not only my first friends in Venezuela but also the first of many steps God would show me as I followed His path. He led me to a doctor who treated Indians along the Orinoco River. He guided me to my first meeting with a tribe of Indians, with whom I stayed for three weeks. He led me to my first job in South America, teaching English to university students in Caracas. And through the man who hired me to teach, He showed me why He had brought me to South America.

"Have you ever heard of the Motilone tribe?" this man, Miguel Nieto, asked me one day. He explained that the primary contact between the Motilone (pronounced *mō-tē-lōn*) tribe and civilization came in the form of arrows. No one had ever learned any of the Motilone language, nor had anyone been close enough to describe their physical culture. These Indians lived in the rainforests of the Maracaibo Basin, nestled in the Andes Mountains on the border between Venezuela and Colombia.

Only major American oil companies had seemed to be interested in that region. Every time their employees entered Motilone territory, however, they were shot at. Great numbers had been wounded by Motilone arrows; many had been killed.

It would have made sense to forget about the Motilones. But I couldn't. A gnawing, troubling curiosity gripped me. And it wouldn't go away, no matter how persuasive the arguments I used against it.

What on earth can I do for a bunch of primitive Indians? I asked myself.

It didn't matter what I thought I could do. In my innermost self I somehow *knew* that God wanted me to go to them.

It wasn't long before I packed up a week's worth of supplies, bused to a small town in the foothills of the Andes, bought a mule, and headed off into the jungle. I was in good spirits, pleased with myself and excited about my new adventure. Two days later, I stumbled upon a cluster of huts that made up an Indian village. I thought these were the Motilones. Soon, however, I realized that they were part of another tribe called Yukos. I lived with these Indians for months, learning more and more of their language and culture. I was ignorant of the ways of the jungle, but through the Yukos I gradually began to acquire the skills I would need to survive.

Finally, I felt I was ready to pursue the mission God had placed on my heart. I asked the Yukos to take me to the Motilones.

Their eyes opened wide with horror. "Oh, no, we don't go near them. They'd kill us," one said.

I insisted.

"Well," the same one said, "there is a Yuko village south of here. Maybe they will take you. You can try there."

And so I traveled from one Yuko settlement to another, trying to find someone who would introduce me to the Motilones. In July of 1962, I met a strong young Indian with a reputation for being willing to do anything if he could gain from it. Since the Yukos loved bright things, I convinced him to take me by offering him a necklace made from the zipper of my worn-out trousers.

We left with six other Yukos the next day, keeping up a grinding pace for a week. Finally we reached a ridge that I was told overlooked a Motilone home.

Suddenly all the Yukos stopped and raised their heads as if to sniff the wind. They stood like statues. I hadn't heard a sound, but I stood still, too, listening to my breath come hard and loud—too loud, I thought. I heard nothing else.

Then, as if in one motion, all the Yukos broke into a run, back the way we'd come. I stood stunned for a moment, then, clumsily, ran after them, wondering what I was running for. I ran straight into some vines, fell flat on my face, scrambled up, and got tangled in the vines again. Suddenly a searing pain bit into my thigh, and my whole body went limp.

I'd been shot by an arrow. I had finally found the Motilones—or rather, they had found me.

The Motilones did not kill me, but I was their prisoner. I spent a miserable month confined to a mat in their communal longhouse, a forty-foot-high brown mound of palm poles and thatch that looked like a beehive from the outside. My leg was infected where the arrow had entered. The glands in my groin were swollen. I was weak. I had diarrhea.

> Suddenly all the Yukos stopped and raised
> their heads as if to sniff the wind. They
> stood like statues. I hadn't heard a sound,
> but I stood still, too.

My initial impressions of the Motilones were not favorable. At first, I was offered nothing to eat. The Motilone women ignored me. Most of the men seemed cruel. They poked me with arrows and snickered when I jumped. Only one Indian showed me any kindness, a fellow with a loud, distinctive laugh and a little scar by the side of his mouth. Every day when he came back from hunting, he grinned and said something to me. Sometimes he brought me food.

My condition grew worse. I decided that I would not survive without medical help. That night, when the Indians were asleep, I sneaked out of the home, found a river, and headed upstream toward the mountains. Feverish, hungry, and scared, I walked for days. Finally, when I was nearly ready to give up, I stumbled across a pair of colonists felling a tree. I learned that I had crossed the border and was now in Colombia. I had escaped the Motilones.

But I did not stay away long. I began to regain my strength and eventually made my way to Colombia's capital city, Bogotá. I enjoyed Bogotá immensely. It was wonderful to be able to talk intelligibly with people again. Yet as my health returned, I found myself thinking more and more about the Motilones. When asked about my adventures, I would describe the Motilone people and the way they lived rather than what had happened to me. It didn't make sense, in terms of what I'd gone through with them, but I loved these people for who they were. God had led me there, and I realized that God would lead me back.

Soon I met an oil company executive who offered to put me on a company plane heading near Motilone territory. I was returning to the jungle.

I camped out in Motilone territory, leaving gifts along the trails to show that I had come in peace. Days stretched into weeks. After two months of waiting impatiently for something to happen, the gifts finally disappeared—replaced by four long arrows in the ground, the Motilone warning that I should run for my life.

Something inside me snapped. God could do what He wanted with these Indians—I'd had enough! I ran to my camp, seized my ax, and ran to the river. I began to chop at a balsa tree. I would make a raft and float out of there.

I worked at a frenzy. Soon the tree swayed and came crashing down into the river. Immediately I moved to a second tree, driving the ax bite deep into its trunk. It too fell. I stepped toward a third.

Then I looked up. There were the Motilones—six of them, their bow strings taut, arrows pointed directly at me. Without thinking I dropped my ax and hid behind a tree. I peered out at them. They didn't seem to have any inclination to hurt me. They were just waiting, holding their bows ready.

Something inside me snapped.
God could do what He wanted with
these Indians—I'd had enough!

I stepped out from behind the tree. I held out my hands, showing that they were empty. My anger was gone. I watched their faces for some sign, my hands shaking slightly.

Slowly they relaxed their bows. One of them stepped forward. I looked closely. He had a small scar on the side of his mouth.

I smiled at him, hoping he'd recognize me. He returned my expression. I grinned more broadly. So did he. He knew me! He spoke a word to the other men. They relaxed. Then he broke into the big, loud laugh that I had known him for on the other side of the mountains. On my first "visit" with the Motilones, he had been the only friendly person I'd encountered. Now, though it seemed impossible, I'd found him again, many days' journey away.

It appeared God still had a purpose in mind for me here.

This time I was accepted into the Motilone community. I was allowed a hammock in the longhouse to sleep in. I was even given a tribal name, "Bruchko," which was as close as the Indians could come to pronouncing "Bruce Olson."

My perspective on the Motilones changed radically from the opinions I'd formed during our initial meeting. I discovered that they were a cheerful people, always joking among themselves, singing, or talking. Every morning, the men went out hunting, while the women stayed behind to begin their work for the day. The children played tag and hide and seek, or made little arrows and shot them at targets of avocado seeds. Later, the men returned with their kill, and there would be a meal—often bocachica fish or monkey meat served on bijau leaves as plates—with everyone shouting back and forth across the community home. Each family cooked its own food and ate it with obvious pleasure. When they were full, their stomachs bulged, and they walked around patting each other's bellies like proud mothers comparing babies.

I was excited to be living among these "primitive Indians," and I worked hard to learn the Motilone language. My progress, however, was maddeningly slow. As the months passed, I grew lonely.

One day a boy of about thirteen brought me some fish. I realized I'd seen him before. He was often assigned to bring me food.

"What is your name?" I asked. It was one of the few Motilone phrases I had mastered.

"Cobaydrá," he said. He watched me eat, a grin on his face the entire time. I wanted to reach out and hug him.

Later that week, Cobaydrá took me by the arm. We ran into the jungle and joined the men for a fishing expedition at the river. Cobaydrá even gave me a spear to try for myself, though my aim was abysmal. From that day on, I had a friend.

A few weeks later, I was asked to follow Cobaydrá, his father, and two other Motilone men into the jungle. Normally easygoing, Cobaydrá appeared tense as we hiked further and further from the longhouse. When we reached a small clearing, we stopped. Cobaydrá's father solemnly produced a loincloth like the ones all the Motilone men wore. I realized with a chill of excitement that this was the ceremony for Cobaydrá to become a man. There was a brief exchange of words and gestures, and then Cobaydrá slipped on the loincloth. He beamed at us.

His father turned to me. "Now that he is a man, he will no longer be called Cobaydrá. He will be called Bobaríshora."

I tried to repeat the name, but it tangled on my tongue. I tried again.

"Bobbishow," I said. That's how it sounded to me. "Bobbishow."

Then I shortened it. "Bobby," I said, and chuckled. The name seemed to fit his pleasant, lighthearted personality. "Bobby" seemed to like it, too.

Being invited to Bobby's initiation ceremony was significant, because only the closest family and friends were allowed to observe the rites. However, I knew enough of the Motilone culture to realize that something was missing. Usually a pact was established with anyone invited. In my case there was none.

I had seen pacts formed before. Part of the ceremony required that the people involved exchange arrows. I wanted to establish a pact with Bobby, and I felt that he wanted it, too. I asked Bobby's brother to make some arrows for me and to arrange the pact.

I was nervous about the ceremony, but it went well. I held out my arrows to Bobby, and he made a show of examining them carefully.

"These are beautiful arrows," he said solemnly. "I accept you as my brother."

Then Bobby handed me his own arrows. They were long and heavy, with beautiful markings. I could see that Bobby, who had been making arrows all his life, had taken extra care with these.

"We are brothers," I sang, looking at Bobby, my face beaming as brightly as his. "We are brothers, and there is nothing in the world that can take us apart."

For the first time in my life, I felt I was in a place where I truly belonged. In the middle of a remote South American jungle, among a people the outside world considered primitive killers, I had found friendship and a home.

I lived with Bobby and the Motilones for the next four years. I learned their language. I introduced medicines that helped heal the Indians. But I made no progress in my true purpose for being there—to introduce the Motilones to Jesus Christ. I hadn't figured out how to tell them about Jesus, to let them see and experience the love of God. I knew that anything I said would be simply dismissed as "the outsider's way."

The answer came unexpectedly during a late afternoon on the trail. Bobby, two other Indians, and I were nearing another Motilone communal home. I began to hear agonized, desperate shouts ahead of us. I veered off the path to investigate.

I came upon one of the strangest scenes I'd ever encountered. A Motilone, one I knew to be a fierce warrior, stood in front of a hole at least six feet deep, shouting, "God, God, come out of the hole!"

Another Indian climbed to the top of the jungle canopy to identify himself with the horizon. In his mouth, he carried the buds of tree leaves—a Motilone symbol of unfolding life—and shouted, "God, God, come from the horizon!"

Bobby explained that the first man's brother had died from a snakebite, far from his home. According to Motilone tradition, that meant his "language"—his spirit, his life—could never go to God beyond the horizon. Now the man was trying to look for God, to get Him to bring his brother's language back to live in his body.

There was a hopeless tone to Bobby's words, but it gave me a shiver of excitement. *This* was why God had brought me to the jungle and allowed me to live. I was here to share with the Motilones where they could find God. Perhaps, after all these years, this was an opportunity God had arranged. It seemed too much to expect.

I spoke to the grief-stricken warrior. He told me about a false prophet the Motilones had followed, whose promises had led them away from God. "It was many years ago, before anyone here was born," he said quietly. "The prophet said that he could take our people over the horizon to a land where there was a better hunt. We left God and followed him. But we were deceived. We no longer know God."

There was a hopeless tone to Bobby's
words, but it gave me a shiver of
excitement. *This* was why God had brought
me to the jungle and allowed me to live.

This sparked a lively discussion. The Motilones do not have ancient religious writings or temples, but they have a spiritual heritage, which is passed on through their legends. The man in the tree climbed down and spoke of a prophecy they believed had come to them on the sound of the wind long ago. "Remember the legend about a tall prophet with yellow hair who will come to us carrying banana stalks. Knowledge of life and God will come out of those stalks, and God will show us the way back to Him."

I immediately recognized the similarity between myself and the description of the prophet. The legend presented me with a unique opportunity, but I didn't understand the idea of the banana stalks. One of the Indians walked over to a nearby banana tree, cut off a section, and tossed it toward us.

"This is the kind of banana stalk God can come from," he said.

It rolled at our feet. A Motilone swatted at it with his machete, accidentally splitting it in half. Leaves still inside the stalk, waiting to develop and come out, started peeling off. As they lay at the base of the stalk, they looked like pages from a book.

Suddenly the word raced through my mind. *Book! Book!*

I grabbed my pack and took out my Bible. I held it up and let the pages fall like leaves. I pointed to the leaves from the banana stalk, then back to the Bible.

"This is it!" I said. "I have it here! This is God's banana stalk."

They began to ask questions. Motilone legends had taught them that God created the first Motilone family by cutting open a pineapple. They believed God defended them from His dwelling place in the heavens, and that is where they wanted to go when they died. Their hopelessness about following a false prophet revealed that they knew they were lost from God. But how could I explain the gospel to them? How could I show that God, in Jesus, had become like them to give them a way back to Himself?

Then I remembered another Motilone legend about a man who had become an ant. The man had been sitting on the trail after a hunt and had noticed some ants trying to build a home. He'd wanted to help them make a good home, like the Motilone home, so he had begun digging in the dirt. But because he was so big and so unfamiliar, the ants had been afraid and had run away.

Then, quite miraculously, he had become an ant. He thought like an ant, looked like an ant, and spoke the language of an ant. He lived with the ants, and they came to trust him.

He told them one day that he was not really an ant, but a Motilone, and that he had once tried to help them improve their home, but he had scared them.

The ants said their equivalent of "No kidding? That was you?" And they teased him, because he didn't look like the huge and fearful thing that had moved the dirt before.

But at that moment he was turned back into a Motilone and began to move the dirt into the shape of a Motilone home. This time the ants recognized him and let him do his work, because they knew he wouldn't harm them. That was why, according to the story, the ants had hills that looked like Motilone homes.

As the story flashed into my mind, I understood its lesson for the first time: if you are big and powerful, you have to become small and weak in order to work with other weak beings. It was a perfect parallel for what God had done in Jesus.

But there were so many unknown factors in the way the Motilones reasoned. How could I be sure that I would convey the right thing?

I couldn't. Yet I felt sure God had given me this time to speak. So I took the word for "becoming like an ant" and used it for incarnation. "God is incarnated into man," I said.

They gasped. There was a tense, hushed silence. The idea that God had become a man stunned them.

"Where did He walk?" one asked in a whisper.

Every Motilone has his own trail. It is his personal point of identity. You walk on someone's trail if you want to find him and follow his example. The Motilones call this *yatubay dudu yuna*: following in the footsteps of a chieftain. As the greatest chieftain of all, God also would have a trail. And if you wanted to find God, you had to walk on His trail.

My blood was racing, my heart pounding. "Jesus is God become man," I said. "He can show you God's trail."

A look of astonishment, almost of fear, spread over their faces. The man who had been shouting into the hole looked at me.

"Show us Jesus," he said in a coarse whisper.

I fumbled for an answer. "You killed Him," I said. "You destroyed God."

Every Motilone has his own trail. It is
his personal point of identity. You walk
on someone's trail if you want to find
him and follow his example.

His eyes got big. "I killed God? I did that? How did I do that? And how can God be killed?"

I wanted to tell them that Jesus' death had freed them from meaninglessness, from death and the powers of evil.

"How do evil, death, and deception find power over the Motilone people?" I asked.

"Through the ears," Bobby answered, because language is so important to the Motilones. It is the essence of life. If evil language comes through the ears, it means death.

"Do you remember," I said, "how, after a hunt for wild boar, the leader cuts the skin from the animal and puts it over his head to cover his ears and keep out the evil spirits of the jungle?"

They nodded, listening closely.

"Jesus relinquished His life. But just as you pull the skin over the chieftain's head to hide his ears, so Jesus—when He died—pulled His blood over your deception and hid it from the sight of God."

I stood looking at them, hoping desperately that they would understand. Then I saw on their faces that they did.

I told them Jesus was buried. A wave of grief swept over them. The man who was searching for his brother's language began to weep. It was the first time I had ever seen a Motilone cry. But the thought that God was dead, that they were lost, brought tears and they lamented His death.

I picked up my Bible, opened it, and said, "The Bible speaks that Jesus came alive after death and is alive today."

One of the men grabbed the Bible from my hand and put it to his ear. "I can't hear anything," he said.

I took it back. "The way the Bible speaks does not change," I said. "It is like the papers of your speech that I have. They say the same words one day to the next. The Bible says that Jesus came to life. It is God's banana stalk."

I showed him the page and told him that the little black markings had meaning.

"No one has ever come back from the dead in all Motilone history," he said.

"I know," I replied. "But Jesus did. It is proof that He is really God's Son."

The Indians asked many more questions. Some I didn't fully understand. But I was sure that God had spoken through me. That night I prayed for His Word to touch their lives.

At first there didn't seem to be any response. But one evening, as Bobby and I sat around a fire, he began to talk in a serious tone. "Bruchko, how can I walk on Jesus' trail? None of us has ever done it. It's a new thing. There is no one in the tribe to tell how to do it."

"Bobby," I said, "do you remember my first Festival of the Arrows, the first time I saw everyone gathered to sing their song?" He nodded. "Do you remember that I was afraid to climb in the high hammocks to sing, for fear that the rope would break? And I told you that I would sing only if I could have one foot in the hammock and one foot on the ground?"

"Yes, Bruchko."

"And what did you say to me?"

He snickered. "I told you that you had to have both feet in the hammock. 'You have to be suspended,' I said."

"Yes," I said. "You have to be suspended. That is how it is when you follow Jesus, Bobby. No man can tell you how to walk His trail. Only Jesus can. But to find out you have to tie your hammock strings into Him and be suspended in God."

Bobby said nothing. The fire danced in his eyes. Then he stood up and walked off into the darkness.

Two days later he came to me with a big grin on his face. "Bruchko," he said, "I've tied my hammock strings into Jesus. Now I speak a new language."

I didn't understand what he meant. "Have you learned some of the Spanish I speak?"

He laughed a clean, sweet laugh. "No, Bruchko, I *speak* a new language."

Then I understood. To a Motilone, language is life. If Bobby had a new life, he had a new way of speaking. His speech would be Christ-oriented.

We put our hands on each other's shoulders. I was deeply moved. My mind swept back to the first time I had met Jesus and the life I had felt flow into me. Now my brother Bobby was experiencing Jesus himself, in the same way. He had begun to walk with Jesus.

There was a spiritual revolution that evening among the two hundred-plus members of the Motilone communal home. Everyone wanted to hear more about Jesus.

Over the next few months, Bobby began to change. He became less proud. When he visited other homes, he accepted food immediately instead of forcing himself to go without it to demonstrate his strength, as he had done before.

The time arrived for a new Festival of Arrows. There was excitement in the home. Pacts would be formed. The men would exchange arrows while the women traded aprons. Each of the gifts would reflect the maker's unique talent and craftsmanship. Then both the men and women would have singing contests. They would climb into their hammocks and sing as long as they could, relating legends, stories, and news of recent events. These songs might last twelve hours, without interruption for food, water, or rest.

An older chief challenged Bobby to a song. Bobby accepted, and sang through the night about Jesus, whom the Motilones call *Saymaydodji-ibateradacura*—God incarnate in human flesh. "He has walked our trails," Bobby sang. "He is God, yet we can know Him by walking in His steps."

There was a spiritual revolution that evening among the two hundred-plus members of the Motilone communal home. Everyone wanted to hear more about Jesus. I could see jubilation on their faces. Several days later, I learned that Bobby's song had been repeated at other Festivals of Arrows. The message of Christ was spreading to other Motilone tribes. It was almost more than I could believe.

I had struggled and fought so hard to reach this point. I had risked my life to share God with the Motilones. Frustrated and impatient, I had seen my progress halted many times and doubted whether anything would ever come of my efforts. But despite my stumbling and my sometimes limited faith, God had used me— and Bobby. He had known all along the right time, the proper method.

Now, like water bursting through a dam on the river, He was sweeping me along in His current. I couldn't wait to see where He would take the Motilones and me next.

Chapter 2

Love...and Loss

Bruchko, I want Christ to be foremost for me. I want to yield all to Jesus.

—Bobaríshora (Bobby)

Bobby was changing, and I was deeply concerned. But my concern was a selfish one. I feared that our friendship was about to be permanently altered, that we would never be close again.

The problem was that Bobby was in love.

Atacadara was the prettiest, most vivacious girl in our longhouse. Bobby had let her know through a friend that he liked her. They blushed every time they saw each other. Atacadara was infatuated with Bobby. He was a handsome, strong young warrior, the prize catch, you might say, of the tribe.

One day she had moved her hammock next to Bobby's, and Bobby accepted this. According to Motilone custom, this was all that was needed to signify a commitment between them. Bobby and Atacadara were married.

Her father was angry. He wasn't at all interested in a son-in-law. He wanted his daughter to stay in the family. But she refused.

Bobby was a devoted husband. It wasn't common for Motilone men to share much with their wives, yet Bobby and Atacadara were close from the beginning of their marriage. Bobby's words and caring brought her to Christ. They weren't just man and wife; they were friends. You would hear their low voices murmuring across the communal home until late in the night.

It turned out that my fears about losing my relationship with Bobby were unjustified. Atacadara and I grew to be like brother and sister. When their first daughter was born, I became, according to Motilone tradition, her second father. We were a family.

I felt a greater sense of joy and peace than at any time before in my life. Bobby, Atacadara, and I were constantly together. In December 1966, Bobby accompanied me on a visit back to the United States, meeting my family and old friends. During the trip I was invited to address the Forum on Native Peoples' Affairs at the United Nations, so Bobby joined me there. I bought him a beautiful dark blue suit for a reception afterward, but we couldn't fit his toes into dress shoes, so we found wide tennis shoes and dyed them black. At the reception, we met UN Secretary-General U Thant, who was so taken with Bobby that he invited us back for a private meeting the next day. Later, U Thant wrote of Bobby, "A glimmer of light in a dark world, who can give his people real civilization, the twentieth century's science for their advantage without alienating the people from their ethnic heritage, so beneficial and important for their continued future."[1]

New York City was a wonderful but exhausting experience for Bobby. He described riding in a car as "getting into a stomach and later exiting from it in a different place." He had a blind faith that if he stepped into the street, the cars would stop for him. Fortunately, the cars did stop! He wasn't afraid of what he didn't know. It had been the same for me in his jungle.

So many new sights and discoveries were taxing for Bobby. He spent most of each day sleeping in our room at the Waldorf Astoria. One night, gazing out the window at the New York skyline, he looked particularly lonely. "Bruchko," he asked, "is that moon the same moon that shines over our longhouse in Iquiacarora?" When I said it was, his face brightened immediately.

There were no secrets between Bobby and me. I could see that he was becoming an outstanding young leader of the Motilones. I never had to tell him what to do. In fact, when he came to me for advice, I would tell him that he had to decide for himself. Other young men who had come to know Christ and who had a concern for others began to work with us. A system of leadership developed, and we began to make rewarding progress.

The years passed. While my old classmates from Minnesota experienced the excitement and turmoil of flower power, Woodstock, and antiwar demonstrations in the United States, I spent the end of the sixties and early seventies hunting, fishing, and talking about Jesus with natives in a South American jungle. And I loved it.

By 1971 we had established two health centers in the jungle. Bobby and other Motilones learned how to take blood smears, and stain and test them for malaria under a microscope donated by a pharmaceutical company. Because the Motilones hungered during the seasons when game was scarce, I showed them how to prepare the ground for growing crops. Large fields were susceptible to disease and erosion, so we focused on small parcels scattered in different areas of the jungle. We eventually cultivated acres of cocoa trees and banana plants, as well as corn, beans, rice, pineapple, and more. We introduced livestock—cows and poultry—in order to increase and guarantee access to meat and milk.

While my old classmates from Minnesota experienced the excitement and turmoil of flower power, Woodstock, and antiwar demonstrations, I was hunting, fishing, and talking about Jesus with natives in a South American jungle. And I loved it.

We also organized two schools where Motilones learned not only their native language but also Spanish, so that they would be able to communicate and negotiate with the outside world. The Motilones call their language Barí, which is also the name they call themselves. It literally means "We the people."

All of these changes took place gradually and in consultation with tribal chieftains. I was extremely pleased to see these advances improve the quality of life for the Motilones—or Barí—in ways that essentially preserved their traditional values.

Most rewarding of all, however, was watching more and more of my friends, like Bobby, grow stronger in their identity in Christ.

So much of what was accomplished was the result of Bobby's openness and example. He was not afraid to try something new if it meant improving life for his people. I came to respect and appreciate him even more than before. David said of Jonathan, after he was slain, "I grieve for you, Jonathan my brother; you were very dear to me. Your love for me was wonderful, more wonderful than that of women" (2 Sam. 1:26). I had never understood that. But there is a perfect brotherly love, and this is what characterized my relationship with Bobby. I just wanted to spend time with him and his family and enjoy the things that God had given us together.

Perhaps my favorite moments were after the evening meal, when we would lie in our hammocks or gather around the fire. Bobby and Atacadara would be close together, squatting in the traditional Motilone manner with one leg thrust out and the other bent, the knee touching the ground and the ankle forming a stool of flesh on which to rest. The children, chortling and giggling, would be passed from one person to another. We would sing songs and talk about the things that had happened during the day. If we had a good meal we would rub our bellies, and I might walk over to Bobby and pat his stomach and express amusement. There were jokes and legends of the past, and always stories about Jesus and the things He had done when He had walked the Motilone trails as a man. Sometimes I would take out my Bible and read a passage. Eventually the fires would die down, the air would grow quiet, and the nightly rain would begin to fall. One by one we would drift off to sleep.

On a spiritual level, I believed that I was living in God's will, doing my best to illustrate His love to these wonderful people. And in my heart, I was filled with a satisfying sense of contentment. I'd been blessed to be part of a remarkable friendship and a caring, close-knit family, so different from my experience growing up. It seemed that I had everything a man could want.

Except, perhaps, for one thing.

I had first met Gloria in 1965, in the town of Tibú. The Motilones needed medicine quickly, so I had walked several days through the jungle, rarely stopping even to eat. When I reached Tibú, I was introduced to a young woman who was studying law in Bogotá and who had come down to visit her brother for a few days. Slender and beautiful, she wore jeans and a leather jacket. Her black hair was tied into a ponytail. Her father was German and her mother came from Spain. Although there was an immediate connection between us, I felt it was wise to remain somewhat aloof in my feelings for her. Besides, I was in a hurry to return to the jungle with the medications.

Gloria's brother, a lieutenant in the Colombian army, wanted to see the jungle. He had an eight-day furlough coming up and wanted me to take him and Gloria with me. Though I resisted the idea, they eventually talked me into it.

I led them to the Motilone home nearest Tibú, a two-day journey by boat. We reached the communal longhouse on a fishing day. The Motilones had already constructed dams out of rocks and leaves, and the men were beginning to spear the fish, charging up and down the sealed-off portion of the river, yelling and splashing. Gloria was eager to join them. I had to laugh. I got her a spear. She went into the water up to her waist and walked downriver, peering beneath the surface like a pro. Half an hour later she came back, dripping wet, smiling, with a big fish dangling from her spear. The Motilones loved her for it. No woman had ever gone fishing like that, let alone speared a large fish.

It was a wonderful week. Gloria helped the women smoke the fish, weave, and do all their work. She was infatuated with the Motilone way of life, and the women loved her.

When the eight days were up, Gloria and I stood in the middle of the clearing next to the longhouse. During the week we had both become aware of our developing connection with each other. But our lives were so far apart that it seemed unlikely, even impossible, that we would ever share a future together. As we stood together, there in the clearing, she swung her arm around, as if trying to gather in every aspect of the Motilones' home in the jungle.

"What can I do?" she asked.

"What do you mean?"

"I mean, what can I do? How can I help?"

I didn't take her seriously. Everyone says they want to help.

"You can prepare to be a doctor," I said without thinking about it, "and come in here and help with the health facilities."

I didn't see her again for several years. We had written a few letters; then, largely because I had resolved to be aloof, they had ended.

In 1970 I was in Bogotá, walking down one of the busy streets, when someone poked a book into my back. I turned around. It was Gloria. She was the same girl I remembered, yet she looked older, more mature.

"Where've you been?" she asked in a teasing tone of voice.

"In the jungle, of course," I said.

"Why didn't you write me?"

"Who has time to write? I've been busy."

"Nobody is that busy."

We started down the street. I asked her how her law studies were going. She stopped and nearly cried.

"What's the matter?" I asked, thinking that maybe she had flunked out of law school and was ashamed.

"I'm in medical school now," she said. "You told me that if I wanted to help the Motilones I should go to medical school. I quit law school."

I could barely remember having told her. Now I realized that she was serious about helping.

> There is a perfect brotherly love,
> and this is what characterized my
> relationship with Bobby.

From then on, whenever I was in Bogotá, I stopped to see her and her mother. Gloria and I would go to a Hungarian restaurant that we both liked and would drink coffee and talk by the hour. When I couldn't go to Bogotá I would talk to her on the radio, mostly about the Motilones. We also talked about Jesus.

Gloria was excited that the gospel had given the Motilones hope, but she wasn't sure how that applied to her.

"My ideas aren't the same as those of the Motilones," she said one day while we were in a little café. "I can't understand Jesus. I don't feel I can really know Him."

"But can't you see how wonderful He is?" I asked. "Can't you see how much He loves you?"

She shook her head violently. "I can identify with His sufferings. I've suffered. I saw my father and my brother both die, and I think I know the feel of death. But Jesus—He rose again. Isn't that right? He rose again. I can't rise from my pain."

She put her head down on the table. I put my hand out and held it against her neck.

"You can," I said. "I don't know exactly how. It's always different. But you can rise. Anyone who wants to can, because God will do it for you and with you."

She just kept her head on the table and didn't say anything.

Later we went to one of the cathedrals in Bogotá. In the middle of Mass, Gloria, who had been praying, suddenly threw her arms around me and gave me a kiss. She was crying. "How wonderful! How wonderful He is!" she said.

Not long afterward, Gloria's mother also met Jesus, and there was a family scene, with both of them crying and hugging each other while I looked on, a little embarrassed.

Gloria was close to graduating from medical school. In Colombia, young doctors must perform one year of free medical service in the rural regions before they can begin their professional practice. I knew the secretary of health in Colombia, and I asked him if there was a way for Gloria to serve for a year in Tibú at a small home that had been established for tuberculosis patients.

"I'm sorry, Bruce," he said, "there's no possibility that we could send a single woman there. It's just too rough an area."

I stood still for a second. It seemed as though the air around me and the cars on the street outside and even the world stood still. Suddenly I knew the answer, and it was easy to say it.

"That won't be a problem. We're going to get married."

I think I was more surprised to hear myself say those words than Gloria was later when I asked her.

A few months later, Gloria was in Bogotá taking care of the final details that would satisfy requirements for her medical degree. I was back in my home in the area known as Iquiacarora, eagerly anticipating the impending wedding and the day Gloria would join me in the jungle. I was in love. I felt amazingly blessed.

It had rained all night and was still raining that morning. There were puddles everywhere. I sat at a desk in the health center working on the linguistic materials I'd gathered during my ten years with the Motilones. I planned to publish some papers on the Barí language.

I looked up to see two Indian men standing in the door. They handed me a small packet of five envelopes.

"Where did these come from?" I asked.

They shrugged. "Jorge Kaymiyokba gave them to us to give to you." Kaymiyokba was in charge of procurement in Tibú.

They were telegrams. I opened the first. "She is buried," it said.

Who was buried? It must be Gloria's mother. But no, her mother had sent the telegram. She'd signed it at the bottom.

I ripped open the others. Gloria had been in an accident. Her car had flipped over the edge of a cliff. "Come at once," one of the telegrams said. "We're waiting for you. You must come immediately." But it was dated two weeks before.

And then I read the next telegram. It said that Gloria had died. Her funeral would be in three days.

Gloria was dead.

I threw the telegrams down.

I ran to the house, looking for Bobby.

It seemed as if that day would never end. Sometimes the grief was more than I could take. Other times it all felt unreal. I couldn't believe that it had really happened. I read the telegrams again and again.

> I was eagerly anticipating the impending wedding and the day Gloria would join me in the jungle. I was in love. I felt amazingly blessed.

Bobby talked and sang to me, telling about Gloria, remembering how she had been the first female outsider to come into the Motilone region, recalling how she had speared fish.

My mind went over and over Gloria's death like a machine that wouldn't stop working. I couldn't cry and I couldn't pray, though I tried. But pray for what? She was dead. She'd been dead for more than a week.

The rain continued. By morning, the river was overflowing its banks. Nevertheless, I insisted that Bobby take me downriver, even though he warned that the trip would be highly dangerous in flood conditions.

Bobby was right. As we came into a bend in the river, a large tree trunk struck the side of our canoe and bounced us toward an enormous whirlpool to our right. The current was too strong for us to avoid it. We were thrown from the canoe. We lost many of our supplies; Bobby's money and the Western-style clothes he'd hoped to wear in the city were torn from his body. Yet somehow we survived. We completed the rest of our journey safely.

I spent several days in Bogotá with Gloria's mother. Like me, she was, of course, heartbroken.

On my way back to Iquiacarora, I stopped in Tibú at the house I'd organized for Gloria and me to live in. Tibú, in the jungle lowlands, has a much warmer climate than Bogotá, located high in the Andes Mountains. To help Gloria adjust to the temperature change, I had enclosed a portion of the home with glass windows and installed an air conditioner. Now I sat alone in this house and, for the first time, plugged in the air conditioner. It hummed to life, and in seconds cool air was flowing out of it. Yet to me, the cool wasn't refreshing; it was depressing. I felt estranged in this place. The more this air flowed around me, the more troubled I became. I was anxious to leave, to return to the Motilone longhouse at Iquiacarora. That was home.

When I returned to Iquiacarora, I found new troubles waiting for me.

Bobby met me at the landing strip in the settlement of Rio de Oro, and together we headed upriver toward the jungle interior. We stopped to visit Ayaboquina, a Motilone chieftain. As we talked, we heard the sound of a motorboat on the river below us. Soon we were confronted by a swarthy-faced man named Humberto Abril. He was a colonist. The government had designated all Motilone lands as homesteading territory. Settlers were clearing the jungle to establish their own homes and farms. Some were outlaws, prison escapees who lived on the frontier to avoid arrest. They wanted this territory to be declared a refuge, free from interference by the government or the Indians.

Abril was one of these outlaws.

"I've come to tell you to get off this land," he said. "This is my land. I'm a Colombian colonist. I have the right to claim land for colonization, and I claim this land. You can get off—"

He addressed me, but Bobby interrupted him. "And I have something to tell you." He spoke slowly, calmly, but with great force. "This is our land. It has always been our land. It will always be our land. We have ceded enough land to colonization. Six months ago we ceded lands to you, at your demand, and what have you done? You have sold them, and now you demand more. But we will not give more. We will protect what God has entrusted to us."

Abril began to shake. Spittle came out of the corners of his mouth and made little spots on his red face. Then he put his thumb across the forefinger of his right hand so that it made a cross. He held it toward us. His eyes bulged and his hand shook. He kissed his fingers.

"For God," he said, kissing his fingers again and spitting on the ground. "For the saints." Again he spit, his head jerking to the side so violently it looked more like a spasm than a conscious movement. "For the Virgin Mother." A third time he spit. "And for this cross." He spit again, then—looking straight at us—he held his thumb and forefinger to his mouth and kissed them. His voice grew guttural. "I'll kill you."

Then he screamed it. "I swear, for this cross I'll kill you!"

Later, as Bobby and I continued our journey upriver, I thought about those chilling words. Were they only a curse, only a threat? Or did they mean more?

For some time, Bobby and I had been working together to create a written Motilone language so that we could translate books of the Bible into a form the tribes could understand. We had begun with the Gospel of Mark. Now, though preoccupied by Abril's death threat, we continued with the Book of Philippians.

Settlers were clearing the jungle to
establish their own homes and farms.
Some were outlaws, prison escapees who
lived on the frontier to avoid arrest.

Eventually we came to the third chapter, where Paul writes of his desire to know Christ and be conformed to His image, even to the point of death:

> I consider everything a loss compared to the surpassing greatness of knowing Christ Jesus my Lord.... I want to know Christ and the power of his resurrection and the fellowship of sharing in his sufferings, becoming like him in his death, and so, somehow, to attain to the resurrection from the dead.
>
> —PHILIPPIANS 3:8, 10–11

When I translated, Bobby turned silent and pensive. He clasped his head in his hands and seemed to stare at the ground. I waited, not sure what was going through his mind.

Finally, he peeked at me through his fingers and said in a somber tone, "Bruchko, who is Jesus for you? How important is Jesus in *your* life?" I could see from the look on his face the struggle going on inside. Christ had already become a part of Bobby's life. Now Bobby was deciding if Christ would be *first* in his life.

I watched as this new insight began to awaken in Bobby's spirit. Eventually he spoke, his voice barely a whisper: "Bruchko, I want Christ to be foremost for me. I want to yield all to Jesus. I'll be completed in conformity to Christ's death."

In the danger-charged atmosphere, those words were profound. Bobby was saying, "I don't care whether I live or whether I die; I want to be like Jesus."

I was sitting next to a spiritual giant. My admiration for Bobaríshora, my friend and pact brother, grew even stronger, though I didn't understand at the time how God was dealing with him. Only later would I realize that Bobby relinquished his life to the Lord that day. Only later would I see that Bobby knew, at that moment, he was laying down his life.

More threats from the outlaws arrived by letter, to me and to Bobby. One day one of Abril's associates, Graciano, brought five colonists to the Iquiacarora health center for medical attention. At the same time he delivered a letter. In it, Abril promised to kill any Indian who resisted the settlers' quest for new territory.

I was overwhelmed.

Just how gullible to do you think we are? I thought to myself. *You threaten us, yet you expect us to cure your neighbors cheerfully. Take your treatment and leave here. And don't come back.*

In the danger-charged atmosphere, those words were profound. Bobby was saying, "I don't care whether I live or whether I die; I want to be like Jesus."

Three tension-filled months went by. More threats were made, particularly against the Motilones who had built small homes along the river to show their occupation of the territory.

It was August 4, 1972. Bobby had gone downriver the day before to sell bananas. He had taken two men with him. He was expected back by four o'clock the next afternoon. But four o'clock came, then five o'clock, and still no sign of Bobby. I was concerned. I'd hated to see him go at all.

That evening, Abacuriana, Asrayda, Kaymiyokba, and I got into a canoe to go downriver and look for Bobby and his canoe. On the way we saw four canoes filled with men. Some of them were outlaws, friends of Humberto Abril. I shined my flashlight into their eyes so they wouldn't recognize us. But what were they doing on the river at night?

We passed by the home of Israel, a land settler. Kaymiyokba pointed at the shore and whispered, "Look! Isn't that Bobby's canoe?"

I strained to see, but couldn't tell. There was a canoe with a *paqui-paqui*, the Motilone name for the powerful Briggs & Stratton motor loud enough to drown out all sounds of the jungle. It fit the description of Bobby's canoe, but it couldn't have been his. He wouldn't stop at one of the settler's homes. We floated on by.

We reached a small Motilone home called Saphadana and stopped our canoe on the bank near the communal home. There was no fire inside, no sound. Then I heard a Motilone voice. "Bruchko?"

"Yes."

Aystoicana came running down to the bank. I could barely see his face.

"Bruchko, they've killed Bobarishora. He's dead."

I couldn't grasp what he had said. "That's impossible!" I replied. "We're expecting him in Iquiacarora. Has he passed by here?"

Aystoicana grabbed my arm. "Bruchko, listen to me. Bobby's dead. He's been murdered."

Stunned, I fell onto my knees on the beach. "Where are the two men who were with him?"

"I don't know," he said. "They were badly hurt. They've gone."

I reached out and grabbed Aystoicana's knee, steadying myself. The night seemed covered with red and blue blotches, like wounds. "What happened?" I whispered.

"Bobby was with Satayra and Akasara. They were coming upriver, passing by Israel's farm. Israel was on the bank, motioning and calling them to come over. Bobby was late. He didn't want to stop, but since he'd known Israel for a long time, he thought it might be an emergency.

"Bobby took the canoe over to the bank. While he was leaning over the motor to turn it off, Satayra looked up and saw a man standing behind a tree with a shotgun. Satayra yelled to Bobby and Akasara, telling them to jump into the river. Bobby didn't hear because of the loud motor. Satayra jumped up on the bank and grabbed for the shotgun. As he wrestled with the man for the gun, the man reached for his machete. Satayra let go of the gun to protect himself, and the man used his machete to slit Satayra's arm open from the wrist to the elbow. Satayra tumbled into the river, and Akasara jumped out of the boat to protect himself.

"Bobby tried to get out of the boat, but a blast from the shotgun caught him in the groin. He fell into the river. Some of the pellets hit Akasara in the leg, but he and Satayra swam to the other side of the river. They looked for Bobby, but all they could see was red in the water. Then they saw his body sinking. They also saw eight colonists on the other bank. All had guns. They had been waiting for Bobby. Akasara and Satayra were frightened and ran. They came here and told us."

"Oh, no, no—oh, no," I whispered. I was in shock.

Then I was angry. I made the trip downriver to a temporary military station on the Rio de Oro. I also sent a message to the police. It appeared neither was willing to do anything. They weren't unconcerned, but they were afraid of being attacked themselves.

Bobby couldn't be dead. I refused to believe it.

We spent all of the next day searching for Bobby along the river. I thought he might be wounded and hiding somewhere. Finally, with darkness nearly upon us, we gave up and turned our canoes toward Saphadana. We didn't talk; we were too tired, too sick.

When we reached the point where the Caño Tomás River comes into the Rio de Oro, I saw something floating in the river. It looked like a log. We went over to investigate. It was Bobby, face down.

"Bobby tried to get out of the boat, but a blast from the shotgun caught him in the groin. He fell into the river."

All hope drained out of my body. I felt empty—like a shell. I had convinced myself that this would be like the time in the whirlpool when we'd nearly drowned. Bobby would be alive. We would be reunited.

The river was shallow. I got out of the canoe and turned Bobby over. His face, stark white, was crinkly from being in the water. I closed his eyes with my fingers. He had died at once. The shotgun blast had ripped open the lower half of his body.

"God," I cried, "O God!"

Bobaríshora had been a loving husband and father. He had been a leader for his people, the first to know Christ, the first to read and to organize schools and a health center, the first to advocate nonviolence, protect his people against the thieves of civilization, and translate Scripture.

He had been my pact brother. My friend.

Now Bobby, like Gloria, was gone. Though I knew in my head it could not be so, I acted as if God had left me, too. His current, once so comforting, now seemed to have set me adrift. The joy and peace I had sought for so many years and finally found in the jungle were evaporating like the morning mist. I had intended to share God's love with the Motilones; instead, it seemed, I had brought only pain and the closeness of death.

I wished that I could leave as well. I wanted to join Bobby and Gloria. I thought that death would be an escape, and much preferred to this agony.

Yet I was here, alive. For me, there was still a place on this planet.

Somehow, I had to go on.

Chapter 3
Fertile Soil

May our lives be fertile soil so that Bobaríshora's seed may grow in us.
May his death become a great tree growing in our soil, so that we can live
as he did, helping each other and learning to love.

—ODO

On the evening we found Bobby in the river, we carried his lifeless form upriver to the longhouse. In keeping with Motilone tradition, my hammock was wrapped around his body, each end folded over and tied together with vines. Warriors fixed the hammock into the highest branches of the jungle canopy. In the morning, the vultures began swooping down from the sky to devour Bobby's body.

I remembered when I had thought this ceremony cold and cruel. I believed placing someone in a box, putting him in a hole, and covering him with dirt was better than tying him high in a tree to be carried off into the sky. But now I knew what the ceremony meant. It meant that Bobby was free to go beyond the horizon.

I only wished that I could go with him.

All that day I watched the vultures circle in the sky and glide in on their huge wings to land in the trees. I thought about everything Bobby had done, about how much he had changed as he grew in his love for Jesus, about how his example had affected everyone in the tribe.

I remembered one of our trips to the higher Motilone territory, not long after the birth of Bobby's first son, when we found a boy of five years of age named Odo. The boy's entire family had died in an epidemic. The Motilones believed that if a tragedy fell upon the parents, it would pass on to their children and those who befriended them. As a result, orphans were seldom taken in by other families. Most often, they were left in the jungle to fend for themselves—nearly impossible for a five-year-old.

Odo, however, was surviving. He would make the three-day journey from communal home to communal home, finding someone's leftover food to eat. Yet he was never accepted.

It didn't help that he was an unpleasant boy. He took it for granted that he should be fed and taken care of, and he wasn't thankful when someone did. He also upset things and frequently created trouble.

Since we were just passing through on the day we ran across Odo, I didn't think much about him. But Bobby did. A couple of days later, when it was time to continue our journey, he told me that he would be bringing Odo along.

"What for, Bobby? He'll just get in the way."

"He needs somebody," Bobby said. "Maybe if he comes with us he can help us, and we'll be able to help him."

It wasn't easy to put up with him at first. But Bobby's patience amazed me. He never got angry or visibly upset. Within a few weeks I began to notice a change in Odo's attitude. He stayed near Bobby constantly. Instead of being in our way, he actually began to be a help. When we returned to Iquiacarora, Odo came with us and became part of Bobby's family. Whereas before he had been filthy, he began to wash, even though Bobby had never said a word to him about it. Within a few months people were noticing Odo, not for his bad behavior, but for the fact that he was a precocious young man.

Jesus once said to the disciples, "I will not leave you as orphans; I will come to you" (John 14:18). Bobby realized that, just as God adopts us into His family, we must adopt our orphans. Then Odo, in imitating Bobby, also became concerned for others. Soon families in our longhouse started bringing orphans into their midst. It was amazing to see such dramatic changes inspired by one man acting in the spirit of Christ.

As I sat outside the communal home that day, watching the vultures, I kept thinking about Bobby—about all that he meant to the tribe, to his family, to me. A few friends tried to cheer me, but I sat like a stone.

By evening I could stand it no longer. I wanted to be close to Bobby. I rose and walked to the trees where my brother's body rested. There I stood, looking up at the jungle canopy, as if to say a final good-bye.

It was a dark night, the moon hidden by a blanket of clouds. Yet after a few minutes, a soft breeze wafted in and nudged the clouds aside. In the moonlight I could see the hammock swaying gently in the trees, as if someone were rocking a baby to sleep.

A twig snapped, and I looked around me. To my astonishment, I was not alone—I was surrounded. The entire community, some two hundred people, had quietly followed me to this spot. They too had come to pay last respects to their leader and friend, Bobaríshora. We continued to gaze in silence at the gently swaying hammock.

The entire community, some
two hundred people, had quietly followed
me to this spot. They too had come to
pay last respects to their leader and
friend, Bobaríshora.

Odo was among the crowd. Now fourteen, he had been devastated by Bobby's death. I think he felt responsible, believing that the Motilone legend about tragedy shadowing orphans had now come true for him and Bobby.

Yet despite his grief—or because of it—Odo was the first to break the silence of the night. And God gave him a most beautiful, prophetic prayer.

"This night is black," he said in a strong voice, looking up at the dim silhouette of Bobby's hammock. "As black as is this night, so are our hearts. Bobaríshora, my adopted father, is dead."

He was silent for a moment, staring at the thick tree trunk nearest him. He continued in a new, quieter voice.

"God, this is a tall, sturdy tree, with roots that grow deep into the ground. This tree, Lord, is our people. We have lived in this land all our lives, generation after generation. That's why our roots are so deep and the tree stands so tall.

"We tried to follow God, but we lost Him. We followed our own paths beyond the horizon, and they never took us to the place where You reside; they only ended at another mountain peak or at a river's edge. They never took us beyond the horizon, where we would find You.

"Then Bobaríshora found Your path on the trail of Jesus, and we walked in His steps, following a spiritual leader. But God! Where has the trail taken Bobaríshora? Why did that path lead to this place? God, it can't be."

He stopped and stared again at the base of the tree. It seemed the entire jungle was holding its breath, listening.

"This tree is beautiful," he said. "It is covered with large, perfect blossoms that have opened and shine in the sun. Each of us is like one of these flowers.

"But there is one flower bigger and more beautiful than all the rest. It made the most perfect fruit. This was the life of Bobaríshora. He brought us agriculture, and our stomachs were filled. We were dying of sickness, and he brought us healing through medicine. Best of all these things, he showed us the path to walk with Jesus, so that we have reasons for living. We were all excited by this new life.

"But God, it's so black now. A dry summer wind has blown. The branch has withered and fallen to the ground. The fruit, the most perfect fruit, has dried. Its seeds have been kicked into the dark, dark ground. It has died… Bobaríshora has died and left us."

Briefly overcome, Odo paused and swallowed. His voice grew quieter still.

"God, don't let the seed be wasted. Make our lives fertile soil so that his seed may grow in us. Make his death into a great tree growing in our soil, so that we can live as he did, to help each other and love as Jesus loves. Make this grow up in us because of his death. May all our hearts be this fertile soil."

The crowd slowly began to disperse. Then Ocdabidayna, one of Bobby's closest friends, grabbed his head with both hands and fell on the ground. "Oh, Bruchko," he said, looking up at me. "I'm not a man. I'm a baby, a tiny baby. Only babies cry."

His agony shook the Motilones as I had never seen them shaken. The others disappeared into the jungle to hide their own tears from each other.

"Bruchko," Ocdabidayna said, "Jesus brought us onto the trail of life's experience so that all the tribes of the world could know and emulate Him. Bobby is almost like Him. He died for us."

Ocdabidayna's words pierced my grief like an arrow, stirring the tiniest flicker of hope. *Yes*, I thought. *Bobby conformed himself to Christ, just as Paul wrote: "I want to know Christ and the power of his resurrection and the fellowship of sharing in his sufferings, becoming like him in his death…"*

That day we were translating Philippians, Bobby knew. He became like Jesus—in life, and now, more than ever, in death.

Perhaps it must always be this way. Perhaps it is only through death that new life can begin. Life that brings joy to the living and glory to God.

Perhaps.

A few days later, I accompanied the Motilones on a hunt. We were all trying to recover from what had happened. Though the Motilones do not normally show their grief, I could sense their sadness. Many were also angry. Outlaws patrolled the river, and the Indians found a number of trails out of the jungle booby-trapped with shotguns. We were surrounded by the threat of death. I felt as if this black cloud would never go away.

But life had to go on. The tribe had to eat. I wasn't in the mood to hunt and didn't take a bow or arrows with me. But I thought a few hours in the jungle might be good for me.

"Jesus brought us onto the trail of life's experience so that all the tribes of the world could know and emulate Him. Bobby is almost like Him. He died for us."

The hunt was successful. Many of the men ran ahead to the longhouse with monkey kills. As I walked back with several of the tribal leaders, I knew that the women would already be fanning hot coals as they prepared fires for a feast. Normally, this would be a festive activity marked by frequent and boisterous exchanges, but I knew that any conversation in the longhouse this evening would be muted.

Two of the men just ahead of me had been talking to each other as we walked. Now, as we reached a small clearing, they paused.

"We must avenge the death of Bobaríshora," said the taller one, Abrincadura, putting emphasis on each word. "The colonists believe that they can take over our land by threatening and killing us. We must show them they are wrong."

More hunters filtered into the clearing. Seeing that a discussion had started, they squatted one by one in the usual Motilone manner. Soon we were in the semblance of a circle. Abrincadura also sat and continued talking.

He related the saga of Motilone resistance to outsiders. In the 1500s, Alonso de Ojeda of Spain sailed to Colombia and discovered the Maracaibo Basin. The Spaniards came to believe that the frequent lightning in the Maracaibo had the power to turn stone into gold. When Spaniards began settling in the region, the Motilones fought with and turned back five royal expeditions sent to pacify the Indians. It was these Spaniards who christened the Indians "Motilones," which literally meant "people of the short hair."

A few years later, a German company directed by Ambrosio Alfinger looted a fortune in gold from Caribe Indians on the western coast and attempted to transport the gold over the Bobalí Mountains. Motilones ambushed and destroyed the expedition, leaving behind a fortune of incalculable wealth that remains undiscovered to this day. In the early 1800s, as Simón Bolívar, the celebrated liberator of Latin America, led his troops across the Orinoco plains and the Andes, Motilone warriors harassed Bolívar's troops with arrows. And in recent years, when oil corporations sent teams to drill for oil in the border jungle, the Motilones again pitted their arrows against modern firearms.

"Throughout our history, we have had to fight to preserve our lands from invasion by outsiders," Abrincadura said. "Today it is no different. These invaders will only understand our determination to keep our lands if we strike back."

I could see heads around the circle nodding in assent of Abrincadura's words.

The informal meeting continued into the night, each man taking a turn to speak. They'd all been deeply affected by Bobby's murder and had thought hard about how to respond. Most agreed with Abrincadura's position. These men were great warriors. They did not possess the more advanced weaponry favored by the settlers; none carried a shotgun or pistol. If conflict with the colonists erupted into open warfare, many more Motilones would surely die. But they were skilled with bow and arrow, and they knew the jungle better than anyone. They were confident that they would prevail.

A few men favored another approach, however. These few had been deeply touched by Bobby's life and by what they had learned about the life and teachings of Christ. And they saw profound meaning in the prayer that Odo had uttered under Bobby's hammock.

"Odo has delivered a message to the Motilones from above," said Coshyra, a friend of Bobby. "He has spoken a great truth, a discovery made by Bobaríshora: God, in Christ, takes away the need for vengeance. Christ is our redeemer, and we should not kill His creation.

"Even greater than this truth are Odo's words that the seeds of Bobaríshora's life might grow in the fertile ground of our hearts so that we too might learn to love and live as he did, in the example of Christ."

As the debate continued, I found myself waging an argument in my mind. I feared that if the Motilones did not fight for their territory, their lands would rapidly be devastated—by the land settlers, by the oil companies, by government deforestation. Once it began, the encroachment of civilization would be an unstoppable wave. The Motilones would suffer the same fate as that of many native Indians of the Americas.

But how could I tell these people who had just received the redemption of Christ, who had seen the sacrificial example of Christ in the life and death of Bobaríshora, that now they must kill their enemies? Was this the message I'd come to the jungle to deliver?

Another man spoke, boldly calling for the tribes to go to war against the colonists, to purge the settlers once and for all from their territory.

When he finished, it was Adabadora's turn to address the group. In years past, Adabadora had been a mighty warrior. I knew that he had killed and wounded oil company employees on Motilone lands. In recent months, however, I had seen subtle changes in his manner. He was less forceful in speaking out against aggression by the land settlers. Now he spoke in a calm, clear voice.

"It is true that we have fought many times to protect our lands from those who seek to take it for their own purposes. And we have fought bravely."

More heads nodded. Everyone was listening closely.

"But what have we gained from all this fighting?" Adabadora asked. "Have the outsiders left us alone? Has peace returned to the jungle? No. Instead, there is only more fighting. More loss. More death."

Adabadora paused and turned his head slowly, looking each tribal leader in the eyes.

"This is the lesson we must learn from the killing of Bobaríshora: violence engenders violence. We must find another way."

I sat very still, pondering this amazing statement by a Motilone warrior. Only Jesus could have enabled this man to say such a thing to his people.

Another man shifted in his place, preparing to speak. It was Bachibarí. In his eighties, Bachibarí was the oldest and perhaps most revered of the Motilone chieftains. He had demonstrated his wisdom many times over the years. He had been blessed with good health and another quality that commanded great respect among the Indians—foot speed. Despite his age, he could still outrun most teenagers through the jungle.

Now this great chief raised his head and, talking slowly, addressed the other elders.

"When a Barí speaks, his words are absorbed by the animals and the trees. The spirit of the jungle weighs the wisdom in each man's head and the character in each man's heart. The jungle knows what is good inside each man, as well as what is evil. We all know this."

Bachibarí put his head down for a moment, then continued.

"When Odo prayed under the hammock of Bobaríshora, the trees lifted their leaves to worship God in the heavens. The animals walked among us, accompanying us in our grief. God's Spirit in the jungle has bestowed favor on the words of Odo."

> "This is the lesson we must learn from the killing of Bobaríshora: violence engenders violence. We must find another way."

Bachibarí rocked forward and slowly came to his feet.

"I say that, for now, we do not fight. We wait until God instructs us what to do."

"Bachibarí, how are you going to hear God?" The voice was Abrincadura's.

Bachibarí turned to look down at Abrincadura. "Did you not hear the voice of Odo? Was that the voice of a child talking?" He shook his head. "It was God's voice that night. And we will know the voice of God when He speaks again."

With that, Bachibarí walked into the jungle, leaving the rest of us to stare after him.

It was December 1972 when Colombia's Third Congress on Community Development met in the city of Cúcuta, just a few miles from the Rio de Oro. More than one hundred fifty delegates representing every corner of the Republic of Colombia were in attendance, as well as members of the president's cabinet and more than three thousand citizens.

For decades, Colombian newspapers had portrayed the Motilones to their more civilized readers as fearsome, intractable savages. Parents often labeled their rebellious children "Motilones," and unreformed criminals were described as having an "unbreakable Motilone mentality." But in recent years, as news filtered out of the jungle that the mysterious Motilones had adapted some principles of modern civilization into their traditional lifestyle—including innovations in medicine and education—the attitude toward the Indians had begun to change. The press, aware of Bobby's leadership in bringing about these innovations and of his trip with me to the United Nations, had also reported extensively on Bobby's murder. Interest in the Motilones was high.

As a result, an editorial writer for a Cúcuta newspaper suggested before the conference that the Motilones be included. This sparked a debate. Some of the academicians scheduled to attend felt the "primitive" Motilones would be an embarrassment. Others said, correctly, that the Motilones were now sending students to universities in the city. They had left the Stone Age behind and had entered the twentieth century—and wasn't that what community development was all about?

The Motilones were invited. The delegates and general public greatly anticipated this visit from the jungle Indians. They wondered just what the Motilones would say.

"When Odo prayed under the hammock of Bobaríshora, the trees lifted their leaves to worship God in the heavens."

I had agreed to accompany the five-man delegation to Cúcuta. Our journey had taken longer than anticipated, and we arrived three hours late to the convocation. The opening ceremonies had already begun. As the Motilone delegation, led by Jorge Kaymiyokba and Odo, entered the auditorium, there was a stir. The speaker on the platform, the minister of government (equivalent to the U.S. secretary of state), stopped abruptly, and heads turned toward the back of the auditorium. Suddenly the crowd began to clap. Then they rose to their feet. An attendant led the Motilones down the aisle to their designated seats, and still the applause continued. From the back of the auditorium, I looked on with pride at this unprecedented demonstration of respect for my friends.

The minister invited the head of the Motilone delegation to the platform, and both Kaymiyokba and Odo stepped forward. Even from my seat, I could see that both were nervous.

"We of this congress are tremendously moved by the death of your tribal leader, Cobaydrá Bobaríshora," the minister said. "Our lives are challenged by his vision and ambition for his people. We were moved and impressed as the secretary-general of the United Nations wrote of Bobaríshora as 'a light in the darkness of despair, a young man become leader who doesn't tear down his peoples' traditional values, but who has taken the leadership of his nation to bring the people advantages of the sciences within their traditional systems.' How many Colombians have been guests of U Thant, secretary-general of the United Nations? Bobaríshora was! We are honored that this one was of Cúcuta."

The minister stepped back and gestured for one of the Motilones to speak. Odo moved in front of the microphone. Kaymiyokba also stepped forward, ready to translate his words into Spanish.

Looking out at the delegates and members of the press, Odo reiterated the words of his prayer after the death of Bobby, this time not just to the Motilones but to all of Colombia: "May our lives be fertile soil so that Bobaríshora's seed may grow in us. May his death become a great tree growing in our soil, so that we can live as he did, helping each other and learning to love."

Odo paused for a deep breath.

For the first time since Bobby's death,
I felt a renewed sense of purpose, of peace,
of hope for the future. God was still
sovereign. His power and love were still
strong. He would show me the way.

"In our jungle there are many trails. A stranger to the jungle is always lost because he does not know the trails. Our nation, the Barí people, was lost when we wanted to walk the trail of God. Bobaríshora brought us to His trail. He claimed to have walked in the footsteps of God. This is a big thing to claim! But we believed Bobaríshora because he was a changed leader. His life was different from all other Motilones, and he brought us to meet God. We too put our feet in His steps on this trail. God brought peace to our stomachs, and today we are complete."

As I sat in the back of the auditorium and listened to Odo speak, my eyes welled up with tears. I missed Bobby terribly. I missed Gloria, too. I had struggled to see any purpose in their deaths, any reason for them to be taken away so soon from me and all who loved them.

Yet here, in this auditorium filled with representatives of government, I realized I was seeing the first fruits of Bobby's life. He had a vision for his people—to help them incorporate advantages of modern society without sacrificing traditional values; to protect his people's right to live on the land God had entrusted to them, while at the same time allowing them to live at peace with their Spanish-speaking neighbors; to complete the translation of God's Word into their tribal language so that God's banana stalk—Scripture—might be shared with all Motilones.

Gloria's dream was part of this same vision—to live and work among the Motilones, using her medical skills to heal the Indians and improve their lives, and to grow in Christ with them.

For the first time since Bobby's death, I felt a renewed sense of purpose, of peace, of hope for the future. God was still sovereign. His power and love were still strong. He would show me the way.

Sitting in the back of the auditorium, I bowed my head and began to silently pray.

O God, I want to rededicate myself to this vision. I want to continue what Bobby has started, what You have made possible through him. I want Gloria's dream of providing medical help for the Motilones to come true. Thank You that so much has already happened. Please let us all realize the prophecy of Odo. Make our lives fertile soil for seeds planted only by You.

Three days later, I was reminded again that the seeds God had planted were already flourishing. Colombia's president, Dr. Misael Pastrana, was presiding over the closing ceremonies at the conference. He presented Kaymiyokba with a Medallion of Excellence in recognition of what had already taken place among the Motilones and what the government yet hoped to accomplish with the cooperation of the Indians in the name of community development.

"Tell me something, Jorge," Pastrana said in front of the entire assembly. "We know that you fought for years against invasion of your territory by the Western world, that you were in conflict with us. What has happened in your community that you are now in dialogue with the government? What has brought peace to your people?"

Kaymiyokba looked at the crowd and replied in Spanish. "It is because we walk in a new trail of life's experience."

Pastrana assumed that Kaymiyokba was talking about the Motilone advances in medicine, tropical agriculture, and education, as well as new legal protections of their territory. He related this to the audience.

Kaymiyokba's brow furrowed. "These are not the reasons," he said. "These tools are a benefit to us. But the change is because our tribe now walks in the footsteps of a new leader."

Pastrana smirked. "Ah, I see. You walk in the footsteps of the missionary, Bruce Olson."

Kaymiyokba shook his head. "No, not Bruchko," he said. "We had to teach him how to speak our language, how to suck the juices from insects, how to survive in the jungle. When he was naked we clothed him. Bruchko is not the leader who brought peace to our people."

It was Pastrana's turn to look perplexed. "Then in whose footsteps do you walk?"

"Saymaydodji-ibateradacura. God incarnate in human flesh. Jesus Christ."

Chapter 4

Menace From Above

At our weakest time, God brought us salvation. We met Jesus in the mountains. We were in anger, but with Him we found love.

—ABAYDORA, MOTILONE CHIEFTAIN

I worked at a small desk, hunched over a portable typewriter, the *clackety-clack* of my keystrokes breaking the silence of the early afternoon. I had met so many people, in the United States and around the world, who wanted to know what was happening with the Motilones, so it was important that I try to keep up with my correspondence while I had the chance. In the next room, Jorge Kaymiyokba was in the midst of an animated discussion with another Indian. Kaymiyokba wanted to go hunting, but his friend was concerned about the weather. Though nightfall was hours away, my view through the window was unusually dark; black clouds had obscured the sun.

It was the summer of 1974. We were staying in a Western-style home we called Buiyocbacbaringcayra, one of two I had purchased a few years ago and given to the tribes. As I typed, I shook my head; it was amazing how much had happened in the two years since Bobby's death.

Back then, I hadn't known where to start. When you tip over a glass of milk on a table, you must react quickly to block the spill. How, then, was I to respond to what was happening? The Motilones were entering a new way of life—moving closer to Christ and adopting a philosophy built around the statement that "violence engenders violence." I wasn't entirely sure that this new approach would be successful, yet God seemed to be speaking to the Motilones. I wondered how I could best serve them while also helping them peacefully preserve the lands they had traditionally maintained throughout their history.

I thought and prayed. Our closest neighbors were the land settlers. Our greatest difficulties were with the land settlers. Humberto Abril and the others responsible for Bobby's death had never been tried for their crime. The courts had never convicted anyone for killing Indians in the past, and they didn't want to set a new precedent this time. Abril had left the area, but other outlaws and colonists remained. Meanwhile, more and more outsiders were moving into Motilone territory, not just men but families. Clearly, if there was to be peace, we would need to start with the land settlers.

The Motilones had made some small steps in the right direction. Humberto Abril's brother Ramón had been helping me with odd jobs from the time before Bobby's death. When Bobby was killed, Ramón felt guilty of the murder and was sure the Motilones would want to take revenge on him. But the Motilones decided that Ramón should not be held responsible for his brother's actions. They allowed Ramón to stay, and he became an even greater help to me, distributing medicines and caring for the canoes.

Refusing to take revenge for Bobby's murder was a good start, but with tensions mounting, I knew that we would need to make peace with the settlers on a larger scale. I began to see that one solution might be a tool we were already employing: education. During the past few years we had established jungle schools for the Motilones. I'd created an alphabet and grammar for the tonal Motilone language so the Indians could read the Bible translations I had begun with Bobby and others and begin to express themselves creatively in writing. The Motilone adults attended these informal schools first; then the youth wanted to learn Barí in its written form. We later added Spanish to the curriculum so the Motilones would be able to communicate with the world outside the jungle.

We had already had discussions about an integrated school, one for both Motilone youth and the colonists' children. The colonists had seen the progress the Indians were making and had asked to be part of the schools. We had planned to teach them two languages as well—Spanish, their native tongue, and Barí, so that the settlers would respect the ways of the Indians.

Those plans were dropped immediately after Bobby's murder. But I began to consider the wisdom of bringing them back.

Beginning with two colonist students, this is exactly what happened. I was their teacher. Some of the settlers were wary initially, but once they saw that we were sincere and not a threat, the children came in increasing numbers. Now we had four bilingual schools in the jungle, three of them serving the Motilones *and* the colonists.

There was more. Years before, I had seen the need for the Motilones to establish some sort of economy. The concept of money was foreign to them, but if they were ever to purchase medicine, pay for educational materials, or travel to and trade with the outside world, they would need funds to support these activities. After some research, I determined that cultivating chocolate would be profitable. I traveled to Trinidad to study the chocolate plants that the British had developed there over two centuries, and I brought samples back to the Motilones. We successfully grafted these with the local chocolate plant and harvested a successful and superior crop in less than three years. Once the cocoa beans were fermented and dried in the sun, they were packed in gunnysacks and transported by canoe and truck to a distributor in Cúcuta.

Through the sale of cocoa beans, the first Motilone cooperatives were born. I had learned something about cooperatives from my father, who, as an executive with the cooperative banks of St. Paul, had created cooperatives in a five-state region. Any Motilone who wanted to participate—by tending crops, packing or transporting the cocoa beans, thatching a roof, or donating commodities—was a member of the cooperative and had a vote on how it was run and how funds were distributed. The more each member "invested," the more profit he was able to reap. I kept the records initially, all on paper. In later years, when the Indians learned accounting at the universities, they took over the bookkeeping and recorded everything on computers.

We didn't make much in the early days, but the cooperatives grew steadily and began providing the tribes with financial resources and independence.

The land settlers observed the success of the Indian cooperatives. Soon they asked if they could join in the co-ops as well, and the Motilones accepted them. This fostered respect and cooperation between the colonists and the Indians.

We harvested more than chocolate. I showed the Motilones how to grow corn, rice, beans, and other crops. These crops filled the hunger gaps between the jungle's wet and dry seasons and during lean hunting seasons. Surplus production also enabled the Indians to store foods and to barter for goods at nearby town settlements. The first purchase I recall was for protection against poisonous snakes—a pair of boots. I chuckled while taking a picture of this young man walking through the jungle, naked except for his loincloth and his tall rubber boots!

> The colonists had seen the progress the Indians were making and had asked to be part of the schools. We had planned to teach them two languages—Spanish, their native tongue, and Barí, so they would respect the ways of the Indians.

I continued typing my report. I was grateful to realize how much good news I had to tell—and how God had known of these intended blessings all along. How was I to know, back in the early 1960s when I met a man named Misael Pastrana, that he would one day be elected president of Colombia? Or that my friendship with him over the years would help persuade the Colombian government to pass a law in March of 1974 declaring more 205,000 acres of jungle territory as an "Exclusive Motilone and Forest Reservation," reversing a decades-long practice of government intrusion on Motilone lands?[1]

There was progress in medicine as well. Even in the years before Bobby's death, we had begun establishing health clinics for the Motilones. Now there were eight; this service was also available to the land settlers. All were staffed by native personnel. Our nurses had learned how to make blood smears, dyeing the specimens in order to isolate and identify the exact form of malarial infection and determine the proper response. In the previous year our medical teams had treated three thousand cases without a single death.

This house where I now sat typing, as well as the other I had purchased, were called *Axdobaringcayra* and *Buiyocbacbaringcayra* by the Motilones. *Cayra* means "house" and is a common ending for the names Motilones give to places. These two houses had been converted into tuberculosis sanitariums. Forty-eight patients were staying here in Buiyocbacbaringcayra and in the twelve small cabins we had built on the property.

Tuberculosis was a terribly dangerous disease to the Motilones—it was introduced to the region by outsiders, and the Indians had no natural resistance to it. It was tuberculosis that claimed the life of my good friend Arabadoyca, the Indian with the little scar and large laugh, the first Motilone to show kindness to me.

At the thought of Arabadoyca, I halted my typing. I had so many memories of this courageous warrior. He was the first Motilone to take the message of the gospel to another Indian tribe. Arabadoyca was also the first Motilone to visit civilization—a trip to Cúcuta. I remembered watching his amazement upon seeing people eat chicken eggs and drink cow's milk—to ingest these animals' secretions seemed unbelievable to him at the time. I thought of my first encounter with the grubs eaten by the Motilones, and I understood the culture shock he was experiencing.

The light bulb was another mystery. Arabadoyca thought the light switch could turn night to day and day to night. He ran from the room every time I flipped on the light to keep from being burned by the sun.

Arabadoyca had only seen his reflection in the river water and did not recognize himself when he looked in a mirror to try and tie his newly acquired necktie. To him, a tall building was a carved mountain and a man riding a mule was some sort of strange, two-headed creature. Another time, he tried to speak to a car as it passed by him, believing that everything that moves is living.

Years later, Dr. Guillermo Valencia, president of Colombia, invited me to come to Bogotá with a Motilone for a personal visit. Of course I had to accept this invitation, but I was somewhat fearful of taking a Motilone into the big city. Arabadoyca had no such fears, however—he volunteered immediately. Before we knew it, he had flown on his first airplane ("Flaps just like a bird"), and we were being ushered into the president's office.

Through my translation, Arabadoyca commented on the bright colors of President Valencia's spacious suite. Then the oversized windows—which Arabadoyca called "hard water"—attracted his attention. He walked over to inspect them closely. Before I could stop him, Arabadoyca cleared his throat and spit on the window.

The president and I both stared at him. Embarrassed, I asked, "Arabadoyca, what are you doing?"

"Spitting through the hard water." Since glass was "hard water," he thought that spit would float through it. When I explained this logic to President Valencia, he thought for a moment and, to my great relief, found the incident amusing.

The president asked if the Motilones have music, and I explained to Arabadoyca that the president wished to hear him sing. So with characteristic Motilone enthusiasm, Arabadoyca launched into a lengthy and beautiful song, with perfectly executed falsettos, designed to bring great knowledge to the president so that he could better attend to the needs of his followers. It also included a prayer to God requesting divine inspiration for the president and a blessing from the tribal leaders.

The land settlers observed the success of the Indian cooperatives. Soon they asked if they could join in the co-ops as well, and the Motilones accepted them. This fostered respect and cooperation between the colonists and the Indians.

When he was done, Arabadoyca addressed the president: "You sing for me, too?"

President Valencia then cleared his throat and sang the Mexican folksong "La Cucaracha." I translated the silly words about a cockroach that cannot walk. Arabadoyca was surprised that civilized leaders did not sing of pacts or of their authority. Noting the incongruity in the meaning of the two songs, the president admitted that Arabadoyca's performance was the superior one. "I can't sing as well as you, Arabadoyca," he said. "That's why you're the son of a great chieftain in the Catatumbo, and I'm up here in the cold mountains of Bogotá!"

More recently, after Arabadoyca contracted tuberculosis, he was taken to a hospital in Cúcuta. When I learned that his condition had worsened, I visited him there. He was unrecognizable. Both kidneys had failed. His eyes were swollen closed, and with shaking, blotchy hands, he attempted to pull down yellowed cheeks so he could see me.

The next day he was even more bloated. In a quivering yet strong voice, he talked of precious memories. He recalled the excitement of killing a giant tapir (a South American species related to the rhinoceros) by himself. Despite his condition, he chuckled, saying the tapir was so huge that four warriors had to help him carry it back to his communal home.

A bolt of pain silenced Arabadoyca momentarily, and he squeezed my hand. Then he continued: "But the best is to have walked in Jesus' footprints on God's trail of life. Right now it is even more clear, and beyond that once-unknown horizon, I see where the trail brings me. I know Jesus, Bruchko. I go, but no evil spirit carries me off. I walk with Him. He's alive. I'll wait for you. He calls me now."

Not much later, Arabadoyca was gone.

I was startled out of my reverie at the typewriter by Armando Echeverri, a medical student from Cúcuta who was serving in the area for a year to complete his degree requirements. He worked mainly in Tibú, but came to Buiyocbacbaringcayra every two or three days to look in on our sanitarium. Some said that we looked like twins. I appreciated Armando's friendship and generosity toward the Motilones very much. In many ways, I felt we *were* becoming like brothers.

A patient in the house had a question for Armando, so I stepped into one of the bedrooms to translate. Afterward, I lingered a moment to watch Armando and his patient. The Indians enjoyed him. He had already learned a few Barí words and obviously cared for each of his patients.

Through the bedroom window, I could see another Indian taking medicine to one of the patients in the cabins. It was satisfying, I thought, to see this land again being used for the benefit of the Motilones. It had not always been so.

This area near Tibú was traditionally part of the Motilone habitat. Two long-houses nearly one hundred feet long, each home for about two hundred people, once sat on high ground adjacent to the Tibú River. It was a rich area for the Indians, providing abundant fish and fertile land for growing yucca roots and many varieties of bananas.

It was also rich in another substance, however: petroleum. Once explorers discovered the abundance of petroleum in Tibú in the 1930s, the North American oil companies quickly followed. By the 1950s, the oil magnates understood that the Motilones would not accept the presence of their machines and drills in the jungle. Once, as we sat across from each other at a campfire, a Motilone chief named Abaydora explained to me what happened.

"A silver, magical flying flute came humming out of the mountain ranges," Abaydora said. "As it hummed, fire flew out of its mouth and licked up our long-house. Our people ran out. From behind the trees, the cannibals had machetes in their hands, capturing our people and slicing into our flesh, eating our people away, until we dwindled to only a few. One cannibal mixed dirt in our blood and wiped it on the back and side of the magical flute. It was red then in our blood, and it still flies over our mountains seeking Barí to fill its appetite."

This was Abaydora's description of an airplane attack. The invaders had bombed the Motilone longhouses, killing two Indians and driving the rest into the mountains. I later was told that invaders had taken the body of one of the dead, a woman, cut it open as though it were a hog, and staked it on poles in the jungle.

This incident was considered a great defeat in the proud history of the Motilones.

"I see where the trail brings me. I know
Jesus, Bruchko. I go, but no evil spirit
carries me off. I walk with Him. He's alive.
I'll wait for you. He calls me now."

The Motilones did not give up their land without a fight, however. Sniper attacks against company employees took a toll. Eventually, the oil companies moved all their employees into a single, more protected camp, which grew into the town of Tibú. They abandoned the individual houses outside the camp.

I did not know the history of the region when I purchased two of these abandoned houses from an oil company in 1968. The price was low, and I thought that they might be of use in the future, perhaps as a place outside the jungle to keep my personal things.

When I showed the houses to the lowland Motilones, they were fascinated by the "new" conveniences. Most saw their first light bulbs, which they described as "fire enclosed within hard water." They encountered electricity for the first time. The act of turning a knob and causing loose water to flow from a pipe was a bit amusing. Most interesting, and most feared of all, was the toilet—whatever went into it was never seen again!

It was only later that I made the connection between Abaydora's words and these two houses on the banks of the Tibú—*Axdobaringcayra* and *Buiyocbacbaringcayra*. Abaydora had been chief of the communal home known as Axdobaringcayra. The Western-style houses were on the same site as the destroyed Motilone longhouses of the 1950s.

When I realized this, my mind flashed back to that night at the campfire with Abaydora. I heard his voice again—not just the words this time, but the pain behind them. Sitting in that modern home built by the marauders of years before, I also felt that pain. The roar of the Tibú River in the background seemed to underline the groans that rose from my soul.

Not long after this moment of understanding, some of the Indians were diagnosed with tuberculosis. I knew that they had to be isolated, and quickly. We brought them to the house at Axdobaringcayra. They looked terrible—thin, yellow in complexion, frequently coughing—and their spirits were even worse. To suffer from this disease, be forced to leave their homes, and have to come to Axdobaringcayra, a place that had become synonymous among the Motilones with defeat, was a terrible blow. Caring for them there, I felt as depressed as the patients.

That is, until Abaydora, the old chief, made an unannounced visit. I didn't know it then, but his brother was one of our patients. This was his first trip back to Axdobaringcayra since he had been driven away so many years earlier.

Along with a small group of Motilones, we walked the grounds together. The jungle had been cleared. Roads crisscrossed the site of a once-fertile yucca plantation. We slowly made our way to a bluff overlooking the Tibú River, where

Abaydora stopped. I wondered what he was thinking. Was he still angry over what had happened here?

Abaydora reached down and pulled a thorny leaf plant up from the ground. It was an underdeveloped, white pineapple plant—perhaps one left over from his plantings years ago? Then he looked toward the horizon, and I thought I detected satisfaction in his eyes.

"After much defeat, my people backed away into the mountains," Abaydora said. "And this was our land of defeat. Now it is *ours* again, and our feet again stand on the land, though we are weakened by death and disease.

"At our weakest time, God brought us salvation. We met Jesus in the mountains. We were in anger, but with Him we found love. He loved us as a mother loves her child—even more than this. Jesus knew defeat and suffering, but this brought victory. God took defeat and made it into salvation!

"Now God takes Axdobaringcayra and its sicknesses, and He will make the ailing His strength. This I know."

Abaydora's words were a prayer and a conviction, and the other Motilones and I were greatly encouraged. The time had come for Axdobaringcayra to be seen as a place of victory once again.

I returned to my typing in the office at Buiyocbacbaringcayra, but not before glancing once more out the window. *How unusual*, I thought. *It's turned almost as black as night.*

Suddenly a tremendous rumble roared down from the heavens. It was so loud that the light fixtures in the room rattled. I could hear excited chatter among the Motilones.

I walked outside into the dark afternoon. The treetops were swaying from a sudden stiff breeze. From our high vantage point I could see into the Catatumbo valley. The entire area was enveloped in black, roiling clouds, as if someone had thrown a living, writhing blanket over the jungle.

Abaydora described an airplane attack.
The invaders had bombed the Motilone
longhouses, killing two Indians and
driving the rest into the mountains.

Suddenly, only a short distance away, the clouds opened up. A funnel burst out of the opening and stabbed the ground. A second later, another dervish emerged.

They were coming our way.

"What are they?" asked Kaymiyokba. He and several other Indians had followed me into the yard. His tone did not betray fear as much as intense curiosity. Tornadoes are almost unheard of in the jungle. I doubted if any of the sixty-some patients, staff, and visitors at Buiyocbacbaringcayra had ever seen one.

"Tornado—a great wind," I answered. "And dangerous. We all need to get back inside."

Already the wind was blowing stronger, whipping leaves and small twigs against our bodies. We moved quickly into the house. I heard Indians shouting to one another: "Look! What shall we do? Where do we run? How do we frighten the storm away?"

The Motilones have their own techniques for dealing with threatening weather. Some will sing songs designed to scare the spirit of a storm away. Others will burn the women's hand-woven cloths in order to blow smoke into the eyes of the storm spirit and drive it back, believing that the older the cloth, the more the storm is placated.

As the winds increased and the tornado bore down on us, this is exactly what the Motilones did. Several launched into passionate song, their voices rising above the cacophony of wind and shouts. Others searched for material to burn, then created their own small fires wherever they sat. Old cloths, towels, aprons, and loincloths were soon ignited. Even the skirts worn by the women, all of them handmade and some exquisitely formed, were removed and thrown into the mix. Despite the severity of the moment, I chuckled to myself at the sight of smoke rising from over a dozen tiny fires inside our modern home.

I had instructed everyone to keep away from the vibrating windows, but now I crept within ten feet of the large front room window to watch the tornado move in. When it was perhaps three hundred feet away, I could see dirt and debris swallowed up into the funnel. Strange undulations moved up and down its quivering shape. The whirlwind spun closer...two hundred feet...one hundred feet. Though it hadn't touched the cabins yet, it ripped away branches from the trees next to them. I worried about the patients in the cabins. Then I felt an odd, physical pressure, as if something were trying to pull me apart.

Suddenly the window in front of me flexed and shattered, scattering shards of glass across the floor. The sound of breaking glass filled the house. The storm was exploding each of the windows right out of their frames.

In the next moment, another sound from above overwhelmed the others: *CRAAACK!*

The wind blasting through the windows seemed to pull me skyward as I looked up. Impossibly, the roof was hovering about ten feet above the house! It had been ripped right off the frame.

Though the roof seemed to hang there for an eternity, it could only have been a second or two. Then it crashed back down onto the house.

I ducked. Chunks of roofing material cascaded down on us, and screams filled the air. I felt as if we were being buried alive.

And then, as suddenly as the storm had arrived, it was over. The funnel had dissipated.

I looked around. The inside of the house was in shambles. Everything was covered with debris from the roof and dirt and leaves blown in through the windows. Yet no one appeared to be hurt.

"Is everyone all right?" I called out.

It was Armando, shaking dust off his shoulder and then looking around with a bewildered expression, who replied first. "Yes," he said. "Yes, I think so."

I rushed to the now-open window frame. The cabins—all twelve of them—were intact! It seemed God had spared us all from what could have been a terrible tragedy.

A man with white powder from the roof sprinkled in his black hair approached me. It was Kaymiyokba. His face was expressionless.

"Bruchko, I think maybe it is too windy to hunt today. We will go tomorrow."

Chapter 5

Respect

When Olson came, he and our leaders began to teach new ways of living through medicine and agriculture.... We learn many good things and so we live better in the jungle.

—KAYMIYOKBA

All of the advances the Motilones had made in education, agriculture, and medicine were significant. I was delighted to see that they were able to use the new concepts I had introduced. But nothing was more amazing than witnessing the delight and fulfilled expectation of a native Indian who confessed faith in Jesus for the first time. This was my true purpose, the real message I had come to the jungle to deliver.

I tried always to keep in mind the words of the apostle Paul that had meant so much to Bobby: "I consider everything a loss compared to the surpassing greatness of knowing Christ Jesus my Lord" (Phil. 3:8).

At the same time, however, I chose to be careful in how I proceeded. It was not an accident that I waited nearly five years to discuss Jesus Christ with the Motilones or that I did not align myself with a specific mission organization, even when I had that opportunity in later years. I had to learn the Barí language, of course, so I could properly communicate the basic tenets of Scripture. But it was just as important that I do so in a way that showed understanding and respect for Motilone history and culture.

When I arrived in Venezuela in 1961, I was troubled that I was not affiliated with a mission organization. I was not accountable to an agency, and at one point I was nearly deported because I had no sponsor. I only knew then that I was following as God led. As time went on, however, I began to see my independence as an advantage. I found myself watching too many well-intentioned missionaries do as much harm as good.

My first contact with Indians in South America came through Dr. Christian, a medical doctor. He allowed me to travel with him to a tribe on the Mavaca River. I was particularly interested in staying in the area because a missionary, Mr. Saunders, served in the area. I had contacted Mr. Saunders from the United

States, and he had agreed to meet me at the airport on my arrival and give me a basic orientation, and perhaps even show me the mission compound in the Orinoco. Except that he never showed up.

My first meeting with him in person was just as disappointing.

"What makes you think you can come down to South America without a mission agency?" he asked once Dr. Christian introduced us. "You just want to come down and impose on us. You think we'll have to take care of you. But you're mistaken. You're on your own."

I was at the mission compound only a short time. The various missionaries were guarded in their approach to me. They did tell me that they were having "a certain amount of success at reaching the Indians with the gospel," but that now there was "persecution of the Christians by other Indians." The Christians had been cut off from the rest of the tribe.

Since the missionaries offered me no accommodations, Dr. Christian dropped me off on the north bank of the Mavaca River with a group of the "persecuting" Indians. We all spoke a broken Spanish, so we had a crippled communication. They allowed me to accompany them when they went hunting, and when I couldn't keep up their pace, someone stayed behind with me. When I tripped over vines and roots, they helped me up. They shared everything that they owned. I ate their food and slept in their hammocks. I couldn't believe these friendly and generous people would "persecute" anyone.

When Sunday came, I suggested to one Indian that we all go to the church, which wasn't far from their camp, and listen to stories about God. He looked at me and frowned. "No, we don't do that."

"Why not?"

"Those Christians, they're strange."

He wouldn't say more, but he did take me to the chief of the village, a big, strong character who snorted with laughter when he was told what I wanted to know.

"Listen," he said, "those Christians don't care about us anymore. Why should we care about them?"

"How do you know that they don't care about you? They're part of your tribe."

"They've rejected everything about us," the chief said. "They won't sing our songs now. They sing wailing songs that are out of tune and don't make sense. And the construction they call a church is square. How can God be in a square church? Round is perfect." He pointed to the curved wall of the hut in which we sat. "It has no ending, like God. But the Christians' God has bristling points everywhere. And now the Christians wear the clothes of the outsiders. Why do we need their clothes? They're uncomfortable."

I thought of the Indian Christians I had seen at the missionary compound. They had been taught to dress in clothes with buttons, to wear shoes, to sing Western songs. It reminded me of the time, when I was a youth in St. Paul, that our Lutheran church missionaries sent a barrel of clothes to Indians in Panama. They wanted to clothe the Indians so they would no longer have to feel ashamed of their nakedness. But when the barrel arrived in Panama, the Indians discovered a pair of scissors in the barrel. When one of the ladies learned how to work the scissors, she cut holes in all the blouses to free the women's breasts from the irritating friction. The Indians really didn't want or need Western clothes.

Is that what Jesus taught? I asked myself. *Is that what Christianity is all about?* What does the good news of Jesus Christ have to do with North American culture? In Bible times there was no North American culture. Were the missionaries making a mistake in their preaching? Of course, it probably made them happy to see the Indians dressed like Americans, singing "Rock of Ages." But was that the only way Jesus could be worshiped?

Later, in my early years with the Motilones, I thought again about these differences in culture. A Western missionary would say that the Indians must be taught to say grace before a meal and give thanks to God. Yet I observed that a Motilone mother, after she pulls up a yucca root from the jungle floor, sings a song thanking God for providing nourishment for her family. I also saw that a Motilone warrior on a hunt, after felling a piping turkey, sings a song of praise to God for supplying food for his family. After the meat and roots are cooked and served for the evening meal, the Motilones do not say grace—not because they are ungrateful, but because they already thanked God when the food was obtained.

Similarly, a Western missionary would say that the Indians must learn to worship God every Sunday. Yet the Motilone counting system included only three numbers—they had no concept of a seven-day week, of a day called "Sunday." In subsequent years, when they learned to count and learned more about the civilized world, they were intrigued by the idea of a seven-day week and Sunday worship. They traveled with me to Tibú to attend church services in the city. But afterward, as I listened to them talk, I discovered that they were perturbed by what they saw. The Spanish-speaking Christians, they said, appeared to be touched by God for one hour on one day each week—and did what they wanted the rest of the week. This was disturbing to the Motilones, who regarded *every* day granted by God as a day of worship. They saw their Spanish-speaking brothers as "lazy" and "undisciplined" spiritually. I wondered: *Who needs to learn from whom?*

In my early days in Venezuela, I observed a mission organization with a huge compound surrounded by fences. It protected the missionaries and their children and staff from the natives. But it also separated them. I thought, *This is not the way to reach the Indians, building square houses and fences. What does this teach about the brotherhood of Christ?*

A few years later, I was again reminded of these thoughts. A missionary and his family expressed interest in joining me in the jungle for a time. I thought I would enjoy having a chance to have some new company and speak English again, and I thought the Motilones would appreciate the chance to spend time with other westerners also. And so we made arrangements. I didn't know what I was getting into.

It took twenty natives to transport all the paraphernalia that Fred, his wife, and his two children brought to the jungle for an eight-month stay at a longhouse called *Bachidicayra*. They brought their own food and soon were cooking beef stroganoff from dehydrated products.

However, the biggest hurdle for Fred's family was the communal housing system of the Motilones. As many as two hundred Motilone Indians live together in oval long houses approximately one hundred twenty feet long by sixty feet wide. Some are as high as forty-five feet tall in their centers with sloping thatched roofs that descend almost all the way to the ground. The central area inside each house is filled with hearths for cooking, and surrounding this area, each family has a designated section in which to live.

Outside the house, a garden is planted in concentric circles around the entire perimeter of the house. Each circle contains a different type of crop in graduated heights, with shortest plants closest to the house and tallest plants, usually banana trees, bordering the jungle perimeter. Each family maintains a pie-shaped wedge of the garden that points toward their living quarters inside the house. Although no boundaries are marked, the families know which section of the garden to maintain through continual harvesting and replanting, and which section of the house to use for cooking, sleeping, and caring for their young.

What does the good news of Jesus Christ have to do with North American culture? In Bible times there was no North American culture.

Within their section of the house, each family strings hammocks in several rows from ceiling to floor. Children sleep closest to the ceiling, followed by grandparents or elderly family members; next come the men, and in the lowest hammocks or on the ground are the women and babies. On the ground beneath their hammocks, the family places mats where they conduct their daily activities by the light that comes in from beneath the bottom edge of the thatched roof. Bows and arrows, crafted by the men with unique personal identification marks, hang on the walls. Tools and other supplies are stored in elaborate baskets woven by the women and hung from the rafters of the house.

At nighttime, large bijau leaves are used to cover openings in the Motilone longhouses and keep out unwanted animal visitors. There are no doors to cover the low entrances at opposite ends of the houses—one facing the sunrise and one facing the sunset—and there are no walls inside to separate the living quarters. Because of this, the curious Motilones often wandered into Fred's section of the home to visit and listen to the voices coming from Fred's radio. This bothered Fred.

"Bruce," he said to me one day, "here I am with my wife and children, and we're glad to be here. But our home is so open, we have no privacy for getting dressed or anything else. Would anyone mind if I built a small room to divide our section of house?"

"Fred, no one cares," I said. "The Indians don't know what privacy is. You just do what you do."

Fred frowned. "We can't do that. It's embarrassing."

And so I asked the chief if Fred could create three walls around his family's section of the house. The chief didn't know what walls were, but he said, "Of course, you can do what you want. Everyone is free to express themselves." Soon after, Fred built three walls around his family's area of the house and hung a cloth over the open doorway. He had his privacy.

Then came the night Fred and his family went to the river to bathe. The Motilones are an intensely curious people. They had enjoyed listening to the radio and debating what the "midget" inside was like. They didn't understand the concept of radio waves and transmissions from hundreds of miles away. So when Fred and his family left for their evening bath, one enterprising young Motilone and his friend decided to investigate.

The two Indians walked into the missionary's section of the home, located the radio, and pried it open. They couldn't find any midgets inside, but they did see something fascinating—a network of wires in bright reds, blues, yellows, and greens. These, the Motilones decided, would make wonderful necklace adornments. They ripped them out and, to cover up their work, replaced the wiring with jungle vines.

The next day, of course, Fred discovered that his radio didn't work. He soon found the vines and was furious. The veins in his neck bulged as he confronted a group of Motilones. He didn't speak Barí, but it was easy to spot the perpetrators—they were wearing necklaces that featured jaguar claws, ocelot eye-teeth, and several brightly colored radio wires. There was an argument. Suddenly, before I could intervene, Fred raised his fist, struck one of the Indians in the chest, and stomped off.

I was mortified. I had invited this man, a servant of God, into the jungle to share his insights with the Motilones and in turn to learn from them. And now he was punching his hosts over a simple misunderstanding.

This incident precipitated an invention that changed the Motilones' concept of the outside world. Fred replaced the curtain at the entrance of his small room with a door made of round wood. And he kept that door closed.

Most of the Motilones had never seen a door before. But they understood its purpose—to keep them out. The initial result was that the two hundred Motilones who had shared the house with him, packed their belongings into baskets and moved out, leaving Fred and his family completely alone for the duration of their stay in the jungle.

The long-term result was that the Motilones never forgot that incident or its lesson: Westerners close doors. We build walls. We protect our children and ourselves. And we often cut ourselves off from the people we are trying so hard to serve.

Years later, I had my own encounter with Motilone curiosity. For two thousand dollars, I had purchased my first desktop computer that could be used in the jungle. It was a lot of money for a missionary who didn't always know if funds would be there for the following month. But it would be an invaluable tool for our Scripture translation work and for keeping track of cooperative and medical records. Since there was no electricity, I had also purchased solar panels for power. Once I brought my desktop system into the jungle, I set it up in a corner of the health center.

Soon, however, I had to leave for a couple of days for a medical mission. When I returned, I saw that disaster had struck.

The Motilones, characteristically, wanted to see what was inside this contraption with the magically glowing symbols. They had stripped the keyboard of its letters and disemboweled the hard drive. My computer was destroyed.

I certainly was not pleased. It had taken much time and money to finally obtain a working computer. But I knew there was little to be gained by slugging the Indians. I blamed myself as much as I blamed them. I hadn't bothered to demonstrate the computer's usefulness and importance. And so I did my best to take it in stride. *At least,* I thought, *my friends now have a new set of attractive ornaments for their necklaces.*

Some months later, I was able to purchase a laptop computer for use in the jungle. This time, I showed the Motilones how it functioned and how it would help me in my work. And once they understood, they respected it and were careful in using it. I had no more worries about finding my computer in pieces.

I feel the curiosity and creativity of the Motilones are among the talents God has given them in order to survive and thrive in a hostile jungle environment. I need to respect that. I am not here to impose my important words and values on the "primitives" or to change their culture. I believe that what God wants from me is an interaction with the Indians leading to a shared sense of humanity, responsibility, and love.

I tried to demonstrate this respect during my early years with the Motilones. It didn't take long for me to realize they were extremely susceptible to a variety of diseases. Once, an epidemic of pinkeye infected nearly everyone in the tribe. They were scratching their eyes and looking miserable. Pinkeye itself wasn't dangerous, but it made the Indians vulnerable to more damaging infections.

I had Terramycin with me that would cure the pinkeye, but the Motilones trusted their medicine woman. She had no interest in trying my Western "potion," even though it was clear that her potions and incantations weren't helping.

If I could convince someone to allow me to try my medicine on them, I could prove that my methods worked and the medicine woman's didn't. But that would put me in competition with her. I knew missionaries often felt that a medicine

I am not here to impose my important words and values on the "primitives" or to change their culture. I believe that what God wants from me is an interaction with the Indians leading to a shared sense of humanity, responsibility, and love.

man or witch doctor was a demon element and had to be eliminated. But that didn't seem to be the case here. The Motilone medicine woman didn't pray to demons. She tried to help her people in the best way she knew.

Then I got an idea. I found a man who had a bad case of the disease. With his permission, I rubbed my fingers in the corner of his eye, then smeared his infection in my own eye.

In five days I had developed pinkeye. I went to the medicine woman and told her that I needed help. She sang incantations for me, just as she had for the others. Naturally, it didn't help me any more than it had them.

So I went to see the medicine woman again. I told her that I wanted her to try putting Terramycin in my eyes while she sang me a new incantation because I was from the outside world. She frowned, but by then she was willing to try something new. She took the tube of Terramycin, applied it to my eye, and sang a new song of healing over me.

In three days my eyes had cleared up, and I felt fine. The medicine woman was convinced that her new song had cured me. But everyone else, of course, was still miserable when she sang the new song over them.

I waited for the right time to speak to her again. The opportune moment came one evening when the medicine woman approached me, her shoulders stooped with fatigue. She said that she was ready to take the "potion" that had cured my eyes and use it on the rest of the people while she sang her new song.

I gave her the Terramycin, and within three days she had cured everyone. It increased her stature in the tribe. She was proud of having been effective with her new chant and her new potion. It wasn't necessary to destroy the role of the medicine woman or demean the Motilone culture. She would become an ally—and a channel for other health benefits for the Indians.

I later used a microscope to show her the effects of disinfectant on germs, which she equated with evil spirits that cause illness. She realized that her chants did not have the same effect and eventually introduced disinfectants to the Motilones. The confirmation of this approach is summarized in a letter written by Kaymiyokba to *El Espectador* and published in the newspaper on November 7, 1971.

> When Olson came, he and our leaders began to teach new ways of living through medicine and agriculture....Now we know of the "outside world" and we learn many good things and so we live better in the jungle. We learn that the animals which live in the earth that cause death, which we cannot see with eyes, are not evil spirits but are microbes and can be seen under the microscope![1]

This sensitivity to the culture also applied to my Scripture translation work in the Barí language. When the Motilones build a longhouse, they go into the jungle to find a special wood called *kiachubana*. When it's green, it's flexible. And when it dries, it is impervious to insects and rot. This extremely strong wood is tied horizontally about four and a half feet above floor level, all the way around the thirty-yard-long structure. This is the foundation of the home. It brings unity to all the individual arcs that make up the longhouse.

In our translation of Scripture, we used the word *kiachubana* to mean adoption, as when Jesus adopts us into the family of God. It indicated the lasting strength of the bond in a manner that made sense to the Motilones.

Our contextualized translation was filled with similar images that the Motilones would understand. Yet it was somewhat controversial. I attended a meeting of translators at the American Bible Society in New York. They were entertaining the idea of a contextualized translation of the Bible and were interested in what I had done, even though others saw this as a new interpretation of Scripture rather than a rendering of God's Word.

In New York, we talked about the problems missionary translators in other areas were having with Scripture such as "Though your sins are like scarlet, they shall be as white as snow; though they are red as crimson, they shall be like wool" (Isa. 1:18). To help the natives understand, because they had never seen a lamb or snow, the missionaries were talking about bringing a live lamb to the jungle or transporting snow to them in an icebox. And as I listened to this discussion, I thought, *They're getting off course. They're going into so many particulars, they're losing the essence of the gospel.*

Later, I had a wonderful conversation about this with Ken Taylor, the founder of Tyndale House Publishers who made his own contextualized translation of Scripture in English. I was delighted with what he had done. I thought it was especially effective in bringing God's Word to young people.

As a result of this translation work, as well as my beliefs and initiatives with the Motilones, I often found myself a target of criticism. Some mission leaders

I simply don't believe that what is sin
from our Western perspective, relative
to the cultural values of the moment, is
necessarily sin in the eyes of God.

did not believe that I could or should attempt to work with the Indians without the sponsorship of a mission organization. Others felt that I was too tolerant of dangerous cultural traditions such as the medicine woman or "promiscuity" among the Indians. It is true that the Motilones lived in communal homes and that they did not sign written documents establishing the roles of man and wife. But promiscuity didn't exist. They recognized and upheld the family unit. I simply don't believe that what is sin from our Western perspective, relative to the cultural values of the moment, is necessarily sin in the eyes of God.

On the other hand, there were several Motilone practices from the early years that did trouble me: abandoning orphans, neglecting the elderly, and failing to share foodstuffs with ailing families. Yet once Christ was embraced by the tribes, these "shortcomings" began to change. I realized it was not my role to impose morality on the Indians, but to bear witness to the resurrection of Christ. The Holy Spirit would instruct and conform them into His image, and Scripture would become authority for His followers. And I saw this happen time and again.

Eventually, as more became known about the Motilones and their growth on many levels, supporters seemed to outweigh my critics:

> Olson has apparently shown that missionary work can be advanced without destroying the culture of the people—that the message of Christ is independent of American cultural values. That faith in Christ redeems to the uttermost.
>
> —KEN MITCHELL, CHICAGO TRIBUNE[2]

> If not for what you have already done, there would be no Motilones anymore—only a few tattered peasants with neither land nor pride. You are pursuing the wisest possible course in educating people to fight their own battles with Colombian national society, while trying to maintain land and preserve a sense of cultural identity. With the strength and energy you have already shown you have performed miracles...Someday I would like to write an article about exactly what it is that makes you so different from all missionaries of this world. Perhaps it could help encourage more of the kind of work you are doing.
>
> —DR. STEPHEN BECKERMAN, DEPARTMENT OF ANTHROPOLOGY, UNIVERSITY OF NEW MEXICO[3]

> Your work among the Motilones is an inspiration to many and a counterbalance to wrong views on Christian mission in general and to missionary work in particular.
>
> —REV. JEAN MALAM, SECRETARY OF INFORMATION, SWEDEN[4]

May I express my appreciation for the publication of *Bruchko* by my friend, Mr. Bruce Olson. I am personally grateful for this opportunity which you have given Mr. Olson to tell the story of the remarkable progress which the Motilone Indians have made in contributing to the economical, spiritual, and social development of my country, Colombia.
—MISAEL PASTRANA, PRESIDENT OF COLOMBIA[5]

Some four and a half centuries after initial contact with Christian Europeans the remote Motilone, a Caribe people of Colombia, are at last entering into a positive relation with the wider society....Not all South American Indians are being exterminated, nor are all missionaries to be discounted in their future.
—DR. HAROLD W. TURNER, SCOTTISH INSTITUTE OF MISSIONARY STUDIES, UNIVERSITY OF ABERDEEN, SCOTLAND[6]

Today's missionaries, churches, and agencies should gorge on Bruce Olson's story like kids chomping on fresh-sliced watermelon. We need this story...because [we're] subjected to misleading propaganda about the failures of missionaries and how they have destroyed indigenous cultures. Bruce Olson's story is the best answer I know to people who gripe, "What's the point of sending missionaries?"
—JIM REAPSOME, WORLD PULSE[7]

I was and still am grateful for these comments. But I try not to put too much stock in them one way or the other. If I know I am acting within the will of God, then I must not worry about the opinions of others. Someone will always criticize. For instance, though some believed I was too accepting of Motilone customs, others felt that I went too far. A French anthropologist, after a visit to the jungle, later complained to the governor of the Colombian state of Norte de Santander, "Olson has ruined the Motilones!" He went on to describe what he found so disappointing: Indians tending livestock and crops, health centers with concrete floors, schools that introduced Western ideas and languages. He felt that the Motilones were better off isolated from all contact with the outside world.

The governor explained that years before he had visited the Motilones and seen many sick children with distended stomachs, as well as Indians suffering from malaria and tropical ulcers. He had also seen the encroachment of the colonists on Motilone lands, reducing their hunting territory.

"I am happy that you found the Motilones with livestock, with clothing and schools and modern medicines," the governor told the Frenchman. "They should be able to partake of our society. They are my countrymen. And when my

> I have learned that if I deliver the message
> of the redemption of Christ in the culture
> He gave them, and if I am sensitive in
> how I introduce modern methods and
> technologies, then I have done my part.

Colombian Motilone has found something better, this means that Colombia is now better!"

Some anthropologists made even more outlandish charges—that I owned a hacienda and large estate in the jungle, that the Indians were my slaves, even that I had murdered Motilones. It stirred up so much controversy that a Swedish author and journalist, Andres Küng, was dispatched to the jungle to meet me and investigate. He summed up the controversy this way:

> Because of his pioneering and often controversial work with the Motilones, Bruce Olson has become the stuff of which legends are made. And like all living legends, he has been at the center of much storm and conflict.[8]

One accusation in particular, the charge that I owned a large estate surrounded by Indians, was particularly on Küng's mind as he traveled with me to investigate. Here is what he wrote of his arrival at Axdobaringcayra:

> After a few hundred yards we come to a clearing. A large white house, surrounded by several smaller ones, can just be made out on a hill not far away. *Exactly as [the French anthropologist] usually describes it, I think to myself. A rich man's mansion in the middle, with the Indians' small houses at a respectful distance. So it was true…Bruce lives the life of a large estate owner right in the middle of the jungle!*[9]

But after entering the house with me and having a look around, he went on to say:

> The house doesn't seem to be only for Bruce. The largest part of it is taken up by an assembly hall, which serves as an office during the day. Three large desks are the only furniture in the room, excepting two book shelves, an easy chair, a couple of rocking chairs, and other simple wooden chairs. The Motilones sit there and watch TV. The next largest room is filled with medicine cabinets and other medical equipment….

When he realized that we would be sleeping in two of the many hammocks strung from the walls of the main room, he confessed:

> I begin to understand that I have done Bruce an injustice by suspecting him of living like a lord in the jungle. He doesn't even have his own room. "His" house is in reality a combination of office, medical stock room, and gathering place for the Motilones.... When I realize this, I also understand how treacherously [the French anthropologist] and others can describe the situation.[10]

Küng wrote these passages in his book, *Bruce Olson: Missionary or Colonizer?*, published in 1977. The book refuted the accusations that had been made against me and went a long way in clearing my name. It even included a letter of apology from one anthropologist who realized he had passed along some of the false claims about me without ever checking to see if any of them were true.[11]

I tend to put the opinions of anthropologists and others aside. For me, the dilemma has always been this: How do I help the Indian without taking away his self-respect or disrupting his culture? The last thing I would want to do is turn the Motilones into beggars, looking for handouts from others because their traditional ways of survival have been taken from them. I have learned that if I stick to my priority of delivering the message of the redemption of Christ in the culture He gave them, and if I am sensitive in how I introduce modern methods and technologies, then I have done my part. It is between the Motilones and God as to how the future will unfold. The Motilones are a part of a wider society, citizens of Colombia and citizens of the family of God. As they contemplate these things, they will choose their own destiny.

Chapter 6

Brothers in Christ

We love Him, because He first loved us. He who loves God, loves his brother also.

—MOTILONE CHIEFTAIN READING SCRIPTURE IN BARÍ

Despite my conviction not to impose my values on the Motilones, there were times—particularly in my early years in the jungle—that whispers of uncertainty nibbled at my ears. I wondered if my decision to wait for just the right moment to discuss Jesus with the Motilones was the correct approach. Would the opportunity ever come? Would they be receptive to my words when it did?

Yet from the day that I used the image of a banana stalk to introduce the concept of Saymaydodji-ibateradacura—God incarnate in human flesh—to the Motilones, God blessed this effort. The Indians continually amazed me with their spiritual maturity. Sometimes I felt I was a teacher among students; just as often it seemed I was the pupil and the Motilones were instructors. Without doubt we were equals, growing together in God's grace.

I fondly recall a visit to the interior of Motilone territory, a day that was in many ways typical of those I spent with the Indians. By the mid-seventies, several of the tribes had purchased or traded for Western clothing through the cooperatives as a way to protect themselves from jungle mosquitoes and other bugs. In the elevated mountain areas, however, the insects were more tolerable; all the Indians remained in their native loincloths. I had recently been to the city of Cúcuta, where violence between government forces and revolutionary guerrilla factions was escalating. For me, the journey back to the jungle was a retreat. I was leaving the confusion of the modern world behind and entering a land where people lived in harmony with their environment and each other. I felt both content and relieved.

The day after I arrived was to be dedicated to fishing, an event I always looked forward to. I spent that morning helping the Motilone men and boys construct a dam on a branch of the Rio de Oro. We gathered boulders and rocks of all sizes from the river. It was already warm; sweat formed on my brow as I lugged a

> Sometimes I felt I was a teacher among
> students; just as often it seemed I was the
> pupil and the Motilones were instructors.
> Without doubt we were equals, growing
> together in God's grace.

forty-pound stone from the river to the site of the new dam. The water, however, was cool and refreshing. After the rocks were in place, we collected huge bijau leaves from the jungle to plug gaps in the dam. Further downriver, the women had built a smaller dam, trapping the fish so they would have nowhere to go when the fishing began.

Fishing and hunting are tasks assigned to the Motilone men, while the women harvest crops and prepare the meals. Because of this, when the dam construction was completed, the women returned to the house to wait for fresh fish to clean while the men gathered our spears—sturdy, thin poles carved from palm tree trunks, between ten and sixteen feet long—and waded in. The men, excited, yelled and charged at the fish before each strike. They rarely missed; soon basketfuls of fish crowded the shoreline. The children were also adept; some collected as many as twenty fish that afternoon. I was not so proficient. I was proud to spear a total of four, and I celebrated each success with a whoop of my own.

Dam-building and fishing are exhausting activities, but the Motilones are a hearty people. One of the men challenged the rest of us to a race back to the longhouse, a distance of perhaps three miles. He graciously allowed me a head start, though I doubted it would do much good.

I ran up the mountain trail, dodging fallen trees and other obstacles on the way. Soon, over the sound of my own gasps for air and the pounding of my heart, I heard some of the Indians just behind. They passed me easily. The Motilones take pride in foot speed; the winner of this competition would garner respect from tribal members.

Finally I reached the summit of the trail and spotted the longhouse just beyond. I thought my legs would fall off and my lungs collapse. I looked back and saw a few racers just behind me. They appeared as worn out as I was, but with a last burst of energy they sprinted past me, burst through the openings into the thatched home, and catapulted into their hammocks. I followed, grateful to give my weary body a rest in my own low-slung hammock. As all vigorously swayed back and forth, the racers sang at the top of their lungs, some offering thanks to the Lord for providing a bountiful harvest of fish. Their praises echoed through the valley.

The women were already burning fires to roast and smoke the day's catch. One turned toward me with a grin on her face. "Bruchko, you caught me baskets of fish?"

I held up four fingers.

"Oh, that many baskets?"

I shook my head, pretending to be sad. "No, that many fish." Several of the women giggled.

Another turned away from her work and asked, "Did you run?"

At this I puffed out my chest. "With all my strength."

Kaymiyokba was quick to clear up any misunderstanding. From his hammock, he announced loudly, "He was the first to leave and the last to arrive." This led to more amusement. I chuckled. The Motilones delight in teasing each other. I enjoyed being included in their banter.

That evening, as the women cooked and smoked the fish and the hammocks were silhouetted by flickering fires inside the longhouse, the warriors told stories of the day's adventures. Everyone, it seemed, was talking at once. I was worn out and falling asleep.

Then, as if it had been prearranged, the conversation abruptly died away. Axdabayducdura, a tall, thin warrior who had accompanied me to Cúcuta, crawled out of his hammock and sat next to his sister at one of the fires. He held a square object, and before I realized what it was, he was reading aloud.

"Let us love one another: for love is of God; and everyone that loveth is born of God and knoweth God," Axdabayducdura said. He was quoting from our Barí translation of the New Testament.

An elder chief left his hammock, sat on a round rock next to Axdabayducdura and his sister, and gently took the book into his own hands. "We love Him, because He first loved us," the chief read. "He who loves God, loves his brother also."

As I lay in my hammock, listening to the words of Scripture amidst the crackling warmth of the fires and the comforting odor of roasted fish, I marveled at the incredible reach of the hand of God. I was in one of the most remote corners of the world, living in a jungle among primitive people who had been considered murderous savages for centuries by the "civilized" world. Yet I was among brothers and sisters in Christ. No one on Planet Earth was beyond the Lord's redeeming grace. Even here, I was surrounded by His love.

I drifted off to sleep, content in my spirit.

When I first encountered the Motilones, they were not a "sharing" people. One family might have done well during hunting season and would have more meat than they could eat. The family living next to them in the longhouse might have fared poorly and would be hungry. Yet the first family would give no thought to handing over their surplus. The excess meat would simply spoil.

That changed, however, when the Indians discovered the compassion Christ felt for all. They began sharing not only their food supplies, but also the good news itself.

In 1967, about a year after the first Motilones had become Christians, Arabadoyca and a small group of other men came to talk to me. They had decided that they wanted to tell the Yuko Indians about Jesus.

I was surprised. The two tribes, their territories separated by a three-day jungle walk bordering dangerous rivers, had been bitter enemies for years. The Yukos knew exactly how to taunt the Motilones. They once braided five-inch jungle thorns with vine cords and camouflaged them on a Motilone trail. Then they threw rocks on the roof of a Motilone longhouse. When the Motilones charged out and onto the trails to give chase, they ran over the thorns. From a safe distance, the Yukos scoffed at their agony and then disappeared into the foliage.

The Motilones, of course, were equally antagonistic. They would organize ambushes of their own. These encounters usually turned deadly. One section of the jungle between Motilone and Yuko territory was named "The Dead Trail" because many had fallen in battle there.

But now Motilones wanted to tell Yukos about Jesus. "Arabadoyca, you can't go," I said. "When they see you coming they will kill you."

Arabadoyca was a brave, confident warrior. Now he was also a man of faith. "I do not think so, Bruchko," he said. "We must do this."

There was another problem. At that time the Motilones didn't understand that there were languages other than Barí. They thought that the Yukos spoke just as they did. But the two languages are unrelated. I couldn't see how they would manage to communicate.

Still, I decided not to restrain or discourage them. I did suggest that they go to the lowland Motilone tribes, who hadn't heard about Jesus, but Arabadoyca was determined to visit the Yukos. A few days later his party left. I was concerned for their safety and hoped it wouldn't be a shattering experience. I prayed that God would comfort them and that any disappointment would be a step toward spiritual maturity.

I marveled at the incredible reach
of the hand of God. I was in one of the
most remote corners of the world.
Yet I was among brothers and
sisters in Christ.

They were gone for several weeks. When they returned, unharmed, I approached Arabadoyca.

"How did it go?" I asked.

He was making arrows, and he looked up at me with his familiar crooked grin. "Wonderful," he said. "They had not known about Jesus before."

"And did they understand?"

"Oh, yes, we told them a great many things about Jesus."

"You spoke to them?"

"Of course." Arabadoyca was a little concerned about my surprise. "How would you have told them?"

"Oh...in the same way. But how do you know they understood?"

Again he looked perplexed. "Why, they told us that they did. They were very excited to hear our news, Bruchko."

"You mean you opened your mouth and spoke to the Yukos, and they understood you and talked to you, and you understood them?"

"Of course."

The Yuko and Barí languages are as different as English and Chinese. You could never understand one from knowing the other. Yet I am sure that Arabadoyca and the others were not imagining things. Lying is almost unknown among the Motilones, and they had no reason to deceive me. I can only conclude that God's Holy Spirit gave the Motilones a message and that the Yukos understood.

Arabadoyca's visit to the Yukos prompted a warming trend between the two peoples. It was not long before the Motilones sent a group of their youth to live with the Yukos for several months to learn their ways and language. The Motilones decided to share their recent advances with the Yukos—cattle, crops, and more. We eventually organized a school for literacy in the Yuko language. Now, when Motilones visit Yukos in their homes in the cool mountains, the visitors are handed tunics to keep them warm. So much has changed.

Most important of all, many of the Yukos follow Saymaydodji-ibateradacura, and His message continues to spread. Despite my lack of faith, the Motilones succeeded with their own missions program.

It was a miracle to me, but nothing particularly unusual to the Motilones. For them, anything God does is expected and normal, no matter how amazing. This was just a continuation of His work.

The Motilones influenced not only other Indian tribes with their newfound faith, but they also had a profound spiritual impact on at least one visitor from the modern world.

Samuel Greenberg, an American anthropologist, contacted me in the late 1960s and asked if he could come to the jungle to study the Motilones. In our conversations, he struck me as an honest man unburdened by preconceptions about what he would find. I agreed to his request.

Greenberg's study had to do with the calories and energy the Indians expended each day. He kept a diary of their activities and a record of what they ate. He also weighed the Motilones' waste after they relieved themselves. The Indians found this threatening, but in another sense amusing, along with his sometimes clumsy efforts to learn their language. Although they did not like the smell of tobacco, they tolerated his pipe-smoking as well.

Then Greenberg decided to visit a Motilone tribe in the mountains. His experience there was less favorable. These natives were unfriendly and purposely gave him the impression he was imposing on them.

Greenberg returned a few weeks later, and this time he asked me to translate the words of lowland Motilone songs he'd recorded. The words spoke about the fruit of the jungle and the adventures of the animals. They also spoke of walking in the footsteps of Saymaydodji-ibateradacura, the first to walk on the trail of life. Greenberg understood that the Motilones were singing about Jesus.

> The Motilones influenced not only other
> Indian tribes with their newfound faith,
> but they also had a profound spiritual
> impact on at least one visitor from
> the modern world.

"Bruce, are these Indians Christians?" he asked in a tone of surprise.

"I'm just translating the words for you," I answered. "You decide."

Greenberg recognized a profound difference in the way the lowland Motilones, who imitated Christ, viewed life as opposed to the highland Motilones, who had not met God incarnate in human flesh. The lowland Indians enjoyed a greater sense of security and joy. They were more self-sufficient and tolerant of outsiders. The highland natives were suspicious of outsiders and less secure in general. They sang incantations to ward off the evil spirits they believed lived in the mountain caves.

This encounter led Greenberg to a point of spiritual reflection. We had several conversations about it. Years later, he told me that he had experienced new life through the resurrection of Christ. The genesis for this remarkable discovery began with his observations among the Motilones.

The influx of the gospel among the Motilones had begun with Bobby. During Bobby's life, because of his words and his example, many of the Indians developed an interest in learning more about Jesus and considered themselves followers of Christ. It was a "people's movement."

Bobby's death gave the Indians much more to think about, however. They began to realize that the choice to follow Jesus was an individual commitment, one that would have vast repercussions for this life and the next. They wanted to study, discuss, and contemplate Scripture with a new earnestness.

Not long after Bobby's murder, one of his good friends, Ocdabidayna, approached me. "What is baptism?" he wanted to know. I explained the historical role of baptism as outlined in Scripture.

"Have you been baptized?" he asked. I said yes. "But we have not. What shall we do?" I did not want to give a pat answer. I said he would need to figure that out for himself. I felt it was important for the Motilones to think through these matters and make their own decisions.

A few days later, Ocdabidayna approached me again. "Bruchko, can you baptize me?"

"I can if you believe in the resurrection of Jesus."

Ocdabidayna inhaled deeply. "Good. I am ready now."

And so we went to the river. I lowered his body under the waters of the Rio de Oro and then pulled him back up to the surface. "You were dead in sin. Now you are breathing the air of new life." Other Motilones, watching this, began asking their own questions about baptism. Soon many were confessing personal faith in Jesus, seeking to express this confession in baptism.

I felt these events were more than just an effort among the Indians to go along with the crowd. They were making real, thoughtful, individual decisions to follow Christ. The "people's movement" was transforming into individual confessions of faith.

Jorge Kaymiyokba was among those who were baptized. I realized just how much this meant to him, and perhaps to all the Motilones, after an incident a few months later.

Armando Echeverri, the visiting doctor from Tibú, needed blood for a Motilone mother who had lost a lot of blood during childbirth. Kaymiyokba and I were at the tuberculosis sanitarium in Buiyocbacbaringcayra during this time. When Armando came from Tibú to check on the patients at the sanitarium, he told us about the Motilone mother who was in serious condition at the hospital. We left at once for Tibú.

The woman's doctor was relieved to see us. After we visited the mother, he took us to a small lounge nearby. "I'm so glad you're here," the doctor said. "She needs a transfusion immediately." I explained that I would be happy to donate, but that my blood type was A positive, incompatible with Motilone blood.

The doctor glanced at Kaymiyokba and, knowing that all Motilones have the same blood type, he said to me, "It's a good thing you brought a Motilone. I'll start the preparations for taking his blood." He left the room.

Kaymiyokba turned to me. "Whose blood are you going to take?"

"Your blood," I said. "Otherwise the woman will die."

Kaymiyokba's faced paled. He took a step backward. "No, you're not going to do that." He turned toward the doorway. I stepped around him quickly and blocked his exit.

> The Motilones had changed from a people who did not even notice the troubles of the family next to them to the point where one was willing to lay down his life for another. Such a transformation was only possible through the grace of God.

"Kaymiyokba, if you don't give your blood, who will? I can't. I have a different blood type."

He didn't understand. He kept looking past me into the hallway, but I didn't move.

"There's only one person who can do this," I said. "You."

Kaymiyokba put his head down. "I don't want to. I can't! I have too many things to do in this life."

I didn't understand his selfish attitude. Too many things to do? Was it that he had a problem with this young Motilone mother? Was he scared of the needles, having never seen them before?

Finally Kaymiyokba moved away and sat down. I left my position at the doorway and took a seat beside him. Neither of us spoke. I am sure he sensed my exasperation over his defiance.

After a few minutes, Kaymiyokba turned to me and spoke in a somber tone. "All right," he said. "I will give my blood."

A nurse arrived and led us into an examining room. She had Kaymiyokba lie on a table. Working quickly, she swabbed his arm and jabbed in a needle. Kaymiyokba closely watched the blood flow out of his arm. Then he looked up at me. His expression was a mixture of sadness and contentment.

"Tell me, Bruchko," he said. "When am I going to die?"

Suddenly I understood Kaymiyokba's reluctance. He thought I wanted him to give his life in order to spare the young mother's! Incredibly, in a matter of a few minutes, he had made the decision to sacrifice himself so that another Motilone could live.

I was so stunned that for a moment I couldn't speak. Then I found my voice. "No, no, you don't die. You are just giving some blood. It will not kill you."

Kaymiyokba's eyes widened. "I'm not going to die?"

"No!"

Relief swept across his face as he put his head down on the table. Every muscle in his body seemed to relax. I grinned at him. As the days passed, we were both pleased to see the young Motilone mother make a complete recovery.

Later, I thought more about the Motilones and what Kaymiyokba had been willing to do. They had changed from a people who did not even notice the troubles of the family next to them to the point where one was willing to lay down his life, almost on a moment's notice, for another. Such a transformation was only possible, I realized, through the grace of God. The Motilones were doing more than paying lip service to the idea of walking on the trail of

Saymaydodji-ibateradacura. They'd been renewed at the core of their being. They lived with changed hearts.

I thanked God that I was a witness to these remarkable events, that I had been allowed to live among these people at such a time. He knew all along, of course, what would happen. I understood His sovereignty more clearly than ever before.

Chapter 7

Finding My Place

Bruchko, you are a member of our community. You would starve in the outside world. They don't speak our language there.

—KAYMIYOKBA

The concept of "family" has always been a complicated one for me. I've had mixed feelings about the term for as long as I can remember.

I grew up in what people today call a dysfunctional family. My Norwegian father was a hard man, dedicated to his job as chief executive officer of a prominent St. Paul bank. He didn't have time for my brothers or me. My Swedish mother was a socialite. Everything functioned around high society and receptions. Appearances were important. When Father and Mother hosted an event at our four-story home, my brothers and I were briefly introduced, then banished to the third floor. Children were to be seen, not heard.

My father was a serious person. I cannot remember joking about anything with him. The strongest feeling I had about him was fear. Mother, on the other hand, seemed mostly indifferent. Like any child, I craved love, attention, and approval from my parents, but this was not how our family functioned. Communication between us was always strained.

I didn't feel I belonged.

For my parents, attending the denominational church was another part of putting in appearances. It was important to be at the second service on Sunday mornings—this was the one all "proper" people attended—but church wasn't something to dwell on the rest of the week. Religion was all right as long as it didn't get out of hand. Balance was the key.

I was taught about God in confirmation classes. I learned particularly about His judgment. But much was confusing and impersonal. I felt no connection to this fearsome God so much like my father.

Then came the night when I was fourteen. I gave my heart to Jesus. It stirred the most astonishing feelings inside me: peace and hope. About two weeks later, I began attending a nondenominational church with my friend, Kent Lange, on

Sunday afternoons and evenings. His father was the minister. Services at the tabernacle were so different from our family's church. Everyone was buzzing about, talking, singing, and clapping. The sermons, often academic, focused on the Bible and Christ's compassion in language that made sense. I loved every minute of it.

My parents did not approve. They had been upset when I first told them about the reality of Christ in my life. I suspected they thought I was trying to be better than them by going to another church.

My father called the people at the tabernacle "Holy Rollers." To him, it was the ultimate insult. Every time I returned from a service he would say, "Well, here's our Holy Roller son back from the kingdom of God. What's the message of God to us poor sinners tonight?"

Despite this hostility, I invited my parents to an evening service. To my surprise, one Sunday night they actually came. I was delighted but also nervous. There was a guest preacher that evening from the South. In the midst of his sermon, he shouted from the pulpit, "Some people call us Holy Rollers. Well, brothers, I'd rather roll to heaven than fly to hell!"

My parents were not impressed. They never came back.

One freezing winter night, after another service at the tabernacle, I set out for home. I always walked the five miles to the church and back. It was later than usual and blustery. As I trudged across lonely sidewalks, the wind swept waves of wet snow into my face. The cold blew up my pant legs and the sleeves of my coat. I wanted to rest but was afraid to stop. I remembered stories of trappers freezing to death because they had stopped to rest and couldn't get up again.

I managed to keep going and finally made it to our front door. I was relieved to be home. I reached for the doorknob and had trouble gripping it. My ice-coated mitten slipped off the cold brass.

I slowly worked the mittens off my numb fingers by using my teeth. Finally I was able to grip the doorknob.

The door was locked.

I tried it again to be sure. There was no question. My parents had forgotten that I was out.

I hated to wake them, but I had to get in, so I rang the doorbell. I watched the window of their bedroom, waiting for the light to go on. It didn't. I rang the doorbell again. No response.

My mother could sleep through that noise, but my father was too light a sleeper. I knew he was awake.

"Father, it's me, Bruce. Come down and open the door for me, please. I'm freezing."

There was no reply. Although I didn't want to, I started to cry, the tears freezing on my face.

"Father, please. It's Bruce. Please let me in."

I looked up at the dark window again. It seemed to stare back at me like a dark, hooded eye. Then I thought of the Langes. I knew they would take me in. But it was two miles to their house, back the way I had come.

"Please, Father," I called and waited. There was no answer. When I couldn't wait any longer, I turned on my heel and ran for what seemed a lifetime. Finally I had to stop. I gulped in huge breaths, the cold air burning my lungs with each gasp.

I made it to the Langes, exhausted and shaking. They got up and gave me a warm place to sleep.

My father had made his point—but it didn't stop me from going to the tabernacle.

Then came the day, when I was eighteen, that I told my parents I wanted to go to Venezuela as a missionary. Our discussion turned heated. They acknowledged that since my "religious awakening," priorities in my life had changed—I was a better student, more conscientious, less prone to argue and fight. But that was no reason to let religion guide my future.

"You don't understand," I said. "I'm looking for my space on this planet. A place of peace. Somewhere that I can be useful to the underprivileged."

My parents felt I was not prepared for such a grand undertaking. But I was more prepared than they gave me credit for. I had studied extensively Latin, Greek, and Hebrew and was president of the high school Latin Club. I wrote a high school term paper in Latin that was later printed in the high school literary publication. I completed numerous Bible studies at the tabernacle. I wrote Sunday school materials for the youth there.

In my junior year of high school, I had begun working at the James Ford Bell Library in Minneapolis, where I handled many original Greek and Latin manuscripts that the professors at the University of Minnesota used during their classes. I had also been a reporter for the local newspaper.

> My parents felt I was not prepared for
> such a grand undertaking. But I was more
> prepared than they gave me credit for.

Not one of my experiences or arguments, however, was enough to sway my parents. My father's word was final: "We'll tie you to a post in the cellar of the basement if we have to, but you are not going to South America!"

Crushed, I said I was going no matter what my parents said. In truth, however, I would not leave without their permission.

Several weeks later, I sat in our living room next to the front window and watched the leaves fall from the trees. I felt a little like those leaves. I wanted to grow, to reach higher and higher, to find God's purpose and place for my life. But instead I was cut off from life. Falling. Dying.

Out of the corner of my eye, I saw my mother slip into the room and sit down across from me. She looked at me for several moments. I kept staring out the window.

"You are a very sad boy," she said finally.

"Yes," I said, turning toward her. "I am sad. I have a dream of going to South America. I think it is God's direction for my life. But my parents say I cannot go."

"Are you that disappointed?"

My answer was almost a whisper. "Yes."

Mother sighed and put her head down. All I could see were blonde curls and her hands folded in her lap. She sighed again.

"Bruce, there's something I've never told you," she said quietly. Her head came back up. "I doubt you remember it. When you were a little boy, about four or five, you became very ill. You had a terrible fever and cough. The doctors didn't know what to do. I thought…I thought you were going to die."

Surprised by this sudden revelation, I said nothing.

"I didn't know what to do myself. And so I prayed to God. I said I would accept anything from Him if He would let you live. I didn't want to lose my son."

Though I could hardly believe it, for a moment I thought I saw my mother's eyes moisten. I held my breath.

"You got better for a while, but then the illness came back again—twice. And so each time I prayed the same thing to God, that I would accept whatever He wanted if only He would touch your life.

"And then when Mr. Lange, the pastor from the tabernacle, was here a couple of weeks ago, he said that he believes your idea of going to South America is coming from God. And I remembered those prayers."

My mother was not a dynamic believer. She had never spoken of God or prayer in this way before.

"Bruce, I think God is taking me at my word," she continued, her voice quavering slightly. "But I...I don't want to give you up."

I was deeply moved, so happy I could not speak. I had doubted it before. Now, for the first time, I knew.

My mother loved me.

She straightened her back and spoke again, her voice stronger. "If you are really determined to go to South America, I will give my approval."

At last I found my voice. "Father?"

Mother nodded. "Don't worry about that," she said. "I will talk to him."

And so I went. My father was not pleased about it, and he refused to support me financially. But he allowed me to leave home. Just before I went, he even provided me with the names of people he knew in Venezuela who had once trained at farm credit banks in Minnesota.

The years passed. I saw my parents only every few years on brief trips to the United States. I brought Bobby along on one of these visits, and they met him and were cordial to him. They still did not understand my passion for life with the Motilones. They eventually accepted that this was my life's work, that I would not be returning to Minnesota to live. But there was still a tension, particularly with Father. I wished that things were different, that I had his understanding and approval.

In the 1970s, I returned to Minnesota for my first visit in five years. Father had just announced his impending retirement from the bank. I received a call from the bank president, who invited me to speak at a reception in honor of my father just before his retirement.

I didn't want to do it. "He is a banker. I am a missionary," I told the president. "We are at two opposite poles."

"Yes, but you have one thing in common," the bank president said.

"What is that?"

"He is your father. And you are his son."

I was deeply moved, so happy I could
not speak. For the first time, I knew my
mother loved me.

I agreed to attend and give a brief speech. It was a gala event at an elegant, downtown St. Paul hotel. Everything was in its place. Many illustrious citizens of the banking community were there, as well as former governors and mayors and other associates of my father.

Eventually I was introduced and given twenty minutes for a speech. I talked about my first experiences in South America and my initial contacts with the Yukos and then the Motilones. I described some of the needs I saw and how I felt that a cooperative system would benefit the Indians. I related how the names that my father gave me, people who had developed a cooperative program involving potatoes in Venezuela, were a helpful resource for me as I advised the Motilones on how to establish a cooperative.

Before I knew it, my twenty minutes were up. I concluded by saying, "This was the beginning of my adventures in South America."

The bank president gestured for me to stay at the podium. "You've only just begun," he said.

"But my time is up," I said.

"I think we would be happy for you to take another forty-five minutes." Other heads at the president's table nodded in agreement.

I glanced at my father. His expression revealed that he was hearing and understanding, perhaps for the first time, that I was not wasting my time in South America. I could also see that he was proud that his colleagues appreciated and were touched by what I had to say.

I continued, relating my observations of Motilone culture and how the Indians lived in balance with their environment. I compared the dangers of living in a South American jungle to living in St. Paul when a bank is coming to collect a loan (this put the audience in stitches). I talked about our program of community development and the progress we had made in medicine, education, agriculture, and preserving Motilone territory.

I also talked, of course, about the spiritual transformation that had taken place in the jungle and the peace of God that not only the Indians but also I myself had discovered. I likened it to a family in the United States. You might go through trials and tribulations, but your family does not abandon you. And you draw a sense of assurance from that.

Later that evening, at home, Father and I again discussed my conversion. "You were only fourteen then," he said. "You were a menace."

"That's true," I said. "But even menaces fear God."

I told him how I felt completely transparent before God that night, how I felt His peace and forgiveness in my life.

"Christ is no longer an historical figure to me," I said. "He is a living being with a spiritual nature, and I follow Him. I felt a peace then, and I still feel it today."

My father was an intelligent man who knew how to debate any point. He could use "logic" to refute anything I said. But he could not dispute the sincerity of my words. Just as he did at the reception, he listened, and the words penetrated his heart. The fact that I had found peace touched him—because he had not. All his pushing and driving and socializing to get ahead in the world had provided financial security and status, it was true. But these were not enough. He seemed to realize that I had discovered something even more valuable.

I sensed our relationship moving beyond father and son that night. We weren't enemies or in competition with each other. Like the moment almost twenty years before with my mother, for the first time I felt that my father actually loved me.

I returned to Minnesota a little over a year later. My father and I sat in the living room. It was winter, and I could see a gentle cascade of snow filtering past the streetlight in front of my parents' home. It was an idyllic scene, like the kind portrayed on a Christmas card. Inside, as we leaned back in cushioned easy chairs, the heater kept us warm and comfortable.

Our conversation was surprisingly warm and relaxed also. Father was in a rare, reflective mood, speaking of things in his life that had meant something to him. He discussed my own mission in life in a manner that showed respect, not contempt. Amazed, I just listened.

He told me about a Lutheran pastor who followed Christ with whom he had been talking recently. Then, almost casually, he said, "I understand your spiritual experience now. I have it as well. Before, I mapped out priorities for my life, things that would provide for my family. And these are still priorities. But they don't satisfy. There is something better. I have found this peace in Christ you talk about."

This was an incredible statement coming from my father. Being a properly composed Norwegian and banker's son, I did not shout or dance or run over to hug him. I simply smiled to indicate how delighted I was to hear this news.

> I sensed our relationship moving beyond
> father and son that night. We weren't
> enemies or in competition with each other.

In my heart, I was happy. Happy for him and happy for our family. Perhaps even more than that, I felt a sudden relief that bordered on exhaustion. It was as if a great battle had ended.

And perhaps it had. For more than thirty years, evil forces disrupted the relationship between my father and me, leaving us only with friction and a terrible void. These forces also helped block him from understanding the change that had taken place in my life, the ability to know Jesus in a personal way.

Now—at last—the fight was over.

It was about six months later, early summer 1979, when I traveled to the city of Cúcuta in Colombia. I had been in the jungle since the beginning of the year. Now it was time to check on what was happening with our Motilone students at the university and to pick up my mail from the outside world.

When I stopped at the post office, I noticed several letters from Minnesota. I sat down and started to read.

Father was dead. He had had a stroke and been taken to the hospital. One of the earlier letters asked if I could come at once. He died in March. Now he was buried and gone.

I was dumbfounded. It was just like with Gloria, this sudden and unexpected news delivered on a piece of paper. Yet my first thought was that he knew the grace of God through Jesus. So it was all right. He had lived a full life. It was proper.

I have learned over the years not to fight death. Death is a fulfillment of life. It is distressing to lose someone so abruptly. When you love a person dearly, you miss him or her every day of your life. In the case of my father, I wondered if we should have talked more, and more sincerely, after his conversion. Maybe other things could have been said.

But the fact that he experienced God's grace at the end of his life changed everything. The knowledge helped bridge the gaps. It was healing.

My mother died several years after my father passed. Though she could not point to a specific moment of conversion, like my father or me, I saw her grow in grace during her later years. She also knew the Lord as her Savior when she died.

I am so thankful to God, so delighted, that Marcus and Inga Olson came to know Jesus. I wonder what it will be like to see and be with them again after I leave this life. I believe it will be a much happier time than our life together on earth. It will be like starting over. We will be a true family—part of God's family.

I was dumbfounded. It was just like with
Gloria, this sudden and unexpected news
delivered on a piece of paper.

The death of my father in 1979 gave me much to think about. The meaning of
family. The battles we sometimes fight with those we are close to. The strength
we derive from family relationships.

Strange as it seemed, I would miss my father. Just as I missed Gloria. I spec-
ulated on what kind of future we would have built together. And of course, I
continued to miss Bobby.

It was later that year that Bobby's daughter, Maria Eugenia Cuadudura, came
to me with questions about her father. She was only three when Bobby was
killed. Now a young preteen, she knew about our special relationship, that we
were like brothers. Atacadara had remarried by this time, so Cuadudura had the
influence of a Motilone father figure in her life. But she also regarded me as her
father. The tribe, in appreciation of the new ideas that Bobby and I had introduced, had taken to calling me *Yado*, which means "rising sun," since his death.
But Cuadudura had her own, more endearing name for me: *Taiga* (papá). And
she realized I would be able to tell her things about her real father that no one
else knew.

Her curiosity was piqued by the discovery of an old skirt. Cuadudura was
looking through a basket of her mother's things that had been tied high in the
rafters of the longhouse. She came across a worn dress with an odd interruption
in the weaving pattern.

"Why did you save this skirt?" Cuadudura asked her mother.

Atacadara's face grew tender. "Because I remember the day when I was weaving it." The women used simple looms, two wooden ribs over two wooden sticks
imbedded in the ground, to weave traditional clothing—canvas skirts for the
women and loincloths for the men. "You were just a little girl sitting in my lap."

"You must not have been a very talented weaver then," Cuadudura teased.
"Look at the mistakes in this pattern."

"Those aren't my mistakes," Atacadara said. "They're yours. You put your
fingers into the threads while I worked. And so I left it that way."

Their conversation turned into a long discussion about what life was like when Cuadudura was very young and how Atacadara and Bobby fell in love. Cuadudura was fascinated. She wanted to know more.

She averted her eyes when she approached me. She was shy, almost embarrassed. "Taiga," she said quietly "would you tell me more about my father Bobaríshora?"

She relaxed when she saw the pleased expression on my face. Of course I would tell her everything. But where to begin?

We talked for hours over the next few days. She wrote everything down in notebooks. It was wonderful for both of us.

At about this time, I received two intriguing communications from the outside world. One was an offer to take a position with a new mission organization that the United Methodist Church was creating, either part time or preferably full time. The other was an invitation to teach on missions in a school of theology in Norway. Both would mean leaving the Motilones and the jungle.

Perhaps it was the recent changes in my own family and the loss of my father. It may also have been the tenderness I experienced with Cuadudura as we talked about Bobby. Though I had lost Gloria, that didn't necessarily mean I wanted to be single for the rest of my life. The idea of a chance for a family, for children of my own, took root in my thoughts.

I had feared overstaying with the Motilones. I enjoyed my background role in the tribe, pushing, helping, guiding. But I did not want to be in the foreground. I didn't want to impose my ideals on them.

I saw that there was maturity among the Motilones. God had set them on a new course, and they were handling it well. Though I was in a great sense of the word the author of these changes, the Motilones did not *need* me. This, I thought, was an opportunity to step away.

I was close to Cuadudura and Bobby Jr., of course. In many ways I regarded them as my own daughter and son. But now I had told Cuadudura about her father, about what he had meant to me and to the entire tribe. In a sense, I had passed on Bobby's legacy. What else could I do for them?

Since I was a young boy, I had yearned
for such a place. This jungle was my home,
the place where I belonged. And these
people were my family.

I was close to so many of the others as well. But after all, I was a tall, skinny, clumsy white man living among a tribe of short, brown, skillful Indian warriors. We had been through much together. But if I was no longer needed…

Yet the thought of leaving also troubled me. If I left, there would be a void in my heart. Could I be complete anywhere else?

I knew I should take my struggle to the tribal elders. That evening I said I had received these offers and that I thought it might be best for me to return to my homeland.

"Homeland? What homeland?" Kaymiyokba asked, his eyes wide.

"Well, the United States or Norway," I said.

"Bruchko, you are crazy," he said. "You are a member of our community. You would starve in the outside world. And you would go crazy there. Who would you talk to? They don't speak our language there."

"Well, I would speak English."

"No, no, you don't speak English anymore. You speak our language," chimed in Adjibacbayra. Others around him nodded emphatically.

"You mean you want me to stay?"

"No doubt," Kaymiyokba said. "We are committed to take the news of Saymaydodji-ibateradacura to our neighbors. Who is better qualified as a guide for this than you? You are a tribal elder. You can't start all of these programs and then just disappear."

Kaymiyokba stood there with his fingers intertwined, twisting them this way and that. He was thinking. Then he stepped directly in front of me. It is hard to be intimidated by a good friend who is a foot shorter, but his expression was such a deep mixture of concern and firm determination that I knew he was serious.

"Bruchko, I am going to tell the Colombian authorities that you cannot leave the country," he said. "You must stay." It sounded like a command, but I realized it was really a plea.

I was moved—and happy. My space in their hearts was secure. I had a place where I belonged, where I could care for others and be cared for in return.

Since I was a young boy, I had yearned for such a place. This jungle was my home, the place where I belonged. And these people were my family.

The next day, I was in the longhouse when Cuadudura came to me, slid into my lap, and give me a long hug.

"I knew you would not leave," she said. "I never want you to leave."

I took a deep breath, gathering in the fragrance of the jungle outside, of the dark orange Bashodi berries being cooked somewhere in the longhouse, and of Cuadudura's straight black hair as she snuggled close. I listened to the cry of a macaw in the distance. And I closed my eyes and laughed.

Chapter 8

Schools in the Jungle

I shall serve my people with my best refined talents, just as my father did. I shall always walk as my father—on the path of life, in the steps of Jesus Christ.

—CUADUDURA

It was August 1986. The outgoing president of Colombia, Dr. Belasario Betancur, had invited four Motilones—Jorge Kaymiyokba, Roberto Dacsarara, Fidel Waysersera, and Daniel Adjibacbayra—and me to participate in the Third Congress of Frontier Policies in Cúcuta. The Motilones, by virtue of their expanding efforts in health services, education, and agriculture—underwritten by the cooperatives and established on lands now protected legally by the Colombian constitution—were an example of what was possible for the native people of the region. Government representatives from across Colombia, looking for ways to better serve all the Indians, wanted to hear more about what the Motilones were doing.

I was seated in a conference room waiting for one of the sessions to begin. A few feet away was the national flag adorned in yellow, blue, and red bands, the latter a symbol for the courage of Colombians who resisted tyrants. As I examined the flag, I thought about the four Motilones who had accompanied me here—young leaders whose fathers would have resisted and perhaps killed any Spanish-speaking people who dared to infiltrate Indian territory. Now here they were, speaking Spanish themselves as part of a government-sponsored symposium in the city, in a dialogue with other "civilized" representatives to discuss the future of the region.

In one sense, these four men were the "best and the brightest," the first leaders of a new generation within the tribes to receive formal educational training. They sought peaceful solutions to problems through negotiation with the outside world. Yet they were also only a small representation of the changes taking place among the Motilones.

Our jungle school system, which began so humbly in 1966 with me as the lone instructor, now included seven schools with Motilone teachers who had been

An Indian, equipped with the tools of language and knowledge of the law, is much more effective than a missionary.

certified by the government. In addition, I hired fifteen Colombian instructors to teach Spanish to those who planned to attend high school in the city. More than 450 students, ages five to sixty-five, were part of this program. These included Motilones, land settlers and their families, and members of other Indian tribes. All were taught two languages—Barí and Spanish.

At first, our jungle schools were not so impressive to look at—perhaps a few wooden benches and a blackboard underneath a straw roof supported by poles— but our students did not care. Most seemed to view learning as a challenge and a pleasure. Because the children helped their parents with hunting, fishing, cultivating crops, and other chores, schools were open all day; children attended when they could and were generally eager to do so.

Selected graduates of the jungle education program were allowed to continue their education through high school and/or apprenticeship programs in Colombian cities. More than fifty Motilones, including the four with me in Cúcuta, had taken advantage of this opportunity by accepting scholarships, which I funded.

Most gratifying to me, none of the students—not even one—who had ventured on to study in the cities remained there. Despite the allure of modern living and its conveniences, all returned or planned to return to the jungle to apply their newly developed talents on behalf of their tribes.

It had not been easy to establish a successful program of education. Securing funds for textbooks and other materials, and later for scholarships, was a continuing challenge. As our cooperatives became more profitable, these provided some monies. But we would not have succeeded without the blessing of financial support and prayer from individuals and church congregations with whom I had come in contact over the years.

Even with this help, we sometimes came up short. But God does provide unexpected blessings. One of these was a chance meeting with the owner of an apparel shop in an upscale department store in Houston. When she noticed me looking at her display, she asked me what I thought of it.

"It's sterile," I said, speaking of the colors and designs of the various pieces of cloth in her display.

"You could do better?" she asked in surprise.

"Yes, I could." I explained that as a hobby I had woven cloths since I was a child. To my surprise, the shop owner invited me to send her examples of my designs. Since then I have sold about forty textiles to this woman for her clothing and upholstery line, and I used the proceeds to fund scholarships for Motilone students in the cities.

This investment has been worth every penny. Each student is a success in his or her own way. Certainly the four young leaders who accompanied me to the conference in Cúcuta had unique contributions to make. Each also had a story to tell.

Jorge Kaymiyokba, about thirty years old at the time, had become one of my closest friends among the Motilones. When he was just three, Kaymiyokba's father, Arabadora, was killed by land settlers. His mother died a few years later from measles, not long after I came to the Indians. No one in the tribe wanted him, and he himself was eager to leave, so I arranged for him to attend boarding school in Cúcuta. He was the first Motilone to study outside of the jungle.

Kaymiyokba was something of a rebel in those formative years. When he returned to the jungle on school vacations, he criticized the tribe's lifestyle and values. He liked to wear black—black slacks, black T-shirt, and black sunglasses. But after Bobby was killed, Kaymiyokba began to change. He accepted Christ in his heart. When he was twenty, he married. Other people in the tribe began to seek out his opinion. He became the moral voice of his people.

In 1979, the Motilones established the Motilone-Barí Community of Colombia Association, which became the autonomous, legal organization representing the tribes to the outside world. The Indians, understanding the breadth of Kaymiyokba's education and leadership abilities and his spiritual maturity in following Saymaydodji-ibateradacura, chose him as the association's first president.

Kaymiyokba's spiritual commitment was tested by a tragedy four years later. He and I returned to his home in Brubucanina after a six-day journey to discover that his eldest son, eight-year-old Chidisayra, had rolled out of his hammock while playing with his younger brother that morning in the longhouse. He had become twisted up in the vines that tied the hammocks to the rafters and strangled to death. After gathering yucca roots and palm nuts in the jungle, Abriquitana, Kaymiyokba's wife, had entered the communal home and found her lifeless son.

None of the students—not even one—
who had ventured on to study in
the cities remained there. Despite
the allure of modern living and its
conveniences, all returned to the jungle to
apply their newly developed talents
on behalf of their tribes.

Both parents were devastated. Kaymiyokba had had so many dreams for Chidisayra—hopes that he too might learn more of Jesus and of the world, showing his people how to blend traditional Motilone values with the advantages of the twenty-first century. Suddenly those dreams were gone.

According to Motilone tradition, a medicine man or woman must determine the "real" reason for a child's death. He weighs any previous negative actions by the parents, as well as taboos believed to be cast on them by the demon *Daphidura*. The violent death of an elder child was most serious. It was considered a foreshadowing of troubles to come. Generations of suffering Motilone parents had run into the jungle in such instances to hide their shame and to offer chants that would appease lurking evil spirits.

I wondered how Kaymiyokba, in his anguish, would respond. As one of the most respected leaders of his people, his actions would set an example for the rest of the tribe. He did shed many tears over his loss—I never saw a father in such pain. But he did not reject Saymaydodji-ibateradacura or attempt to appease spirits with chants. During this terrible time his faith endured.

In the mid-1980s, Kaymiyokba continued to serve his people as president of the Motilone-Barí Association. He was also elected director of the Fraternity of Eastern Colombian Tribal Peoples headquartered at the House of Twelve Cultures in Tibú.

Roberto Dacsarara was in his mid-twenties at the time of the conference. He had attended grade school in the jungle—I was his first teacher—before accepting a scholarship to go to high school in Bucaramanga, a city of more than half a million people and capital of Norte de Santander province. It was a new experience for him. When he first walked on a paved road, he tried to dig a hole in it with his heel.

"The ground here is no good," he said. "It's too hard. You cannot plant corn in it. No wonder they put a city here!"

That was a rare outburst for Dacsarara. Tall and clumsy, he was a reserved, studious young man, given to reflection and reluctant to express himself. At first, Dacsarara struggled in the strange environment. There were so many new things to learn beyond just his studies. The schoolwork itself was also challenging, especially mathematics and the more advanced teaching of the Spanish language. Yet he persevered, and it wasn't long before he was on the dean's list for academic achievement. He graduated cum laude from the six-year high school program (the equivalent of a two-year college degree in the United States).

Once, at a Rotary Club meeting in Bucaramanga, a member of the military stated that he thought it would be difficult for the Motilone students in the cities to ever return to the jungle. When it was my turn to speak, I answered him by quoting from Dacsarara's final high school thesis, written in English:

> Colombians call us Motilones, which means "Short Hair." We call ourselves Barí—a name that means "The People." In the cities there is money. If you have much money, you are wealthy. You can buy food and your stomachs are full. If you have no money, you are poor and you don't eat. In the jungle we never have money. There are no wealthy. There are no poor. In the jungle when we want to eat we pull out a root, or we eat the fruit of the seed, the harvest that we planted and our stomachs are satisfied. In the cities there are many trails that go in many different directions. People are constantly running up and down them, all confused. There are many who claim to know the way. You call them politicians. But there is no chieftain. In the jungle we have a one trail. This trail brings peace to our people, knowledge of how to overcome our difficulties. We walk in the footsteps of a new chieftain, Jesus. Where is the most logical place to live—in the cities or in the jungle?

I also shared that the director of schools, after reading the thesis, had asked Dacsarara, "If you don't have money, and you don't build monuments, what is the value of life?"

Dacsarara replied, "The character of each individual."

After high school, Dacsarara enrolled in law school at Free University in Cúcuta, where he also flourished. He was an "A" student, became a student adviser, and in 1986, during his fifth semester, Colombia's high state magistrate named him the court's representative and coordinator for the Motilone territory in Norte de Santander.

Dacsarara even developed into an eloquent speaker. I had been invited to appear before the Colombian Conference in Cúcuta to help them decide who would administer a portion of Motilone territory. I came down with a throat infection, however, so I asked Dacsarara, who had accompanied me, to speak on my behalf. He related to the legislators that in his childhood, he had helped his people fight back against the advances of the oil companies that were supported by the Colombian government. He had seen friends and tribal elders killed. As a child, only twenty years ago, he had gathered the tools and clothes left behind by company employees as trophies of war.

"Now, however, I stand before you as a lawyer of Colombia," Dacsarara said. "I come as a champion for my people. It is not a time to fight but a time for legislation. We must be allowed to administer our own lands. Your constitution cannot take this right away from the Barí. Would you deny what God has entrusted to us?"

When he was finished, there was no applause, only silence. I had made the same plea on behalf of the Motilones many times. But when I spoke, they merely saw a folk hero who lived a romantic lifestyle. When Dacsarara spoke, they saw a man who, in twenty short years, had stepped from a Stone Age culture into the twenty-first century. They couldn't treat him recklessly. A Colombian was speaking to Colombians, and he was claiming the lands for the first nations. They hung their heads in embarrassment and realized that they had to approve the land for the Motilone people. This proved to me that an Indian, equipped with the tools of language and knowledge of the law, articulating in defense of their territory, is much more effective than a missionary.

The impact on the legislators was indeed profound. Within six months, they decreed that the territory in question would be governed by the Motilones.

Fidel Waysersera, about the same age as Dacsarara but shorter and more agile, was perhaps the most engaging, confident, and outspoken of all the Motilones I had encountered. He was one of those people who could talk to anyone about anything and was very popular within the tribe.

Like Dacsarara, part of Waysersera's duties as a child was to assist in raids on oil company employees. When the arrows started flying and the outsiders ran for cover, Waysersera crept into their camps and shacks to gather any metallic-looking objects he could find. These included machetes and axes, as well as silver safety helmets that were especially useful as bowls for cooking wild turkey eggs.

Waysersera attended our jungle school before earning his high school degree in Bucaramanga. He followed this with a year of apprenticeship training in cooperative administration in the town of Armenia, and then he enrolled in law school at St. Thomas University in Bucaramanga. He became the first Motilone to study in a Western university, graduating in 1985.

Waysersera's forays into the modern world created a crisis for him back home, however. When he returned to the jungle for the long Easter break during his year of apprenticeship, he found that his skills as an Indian warrior had eroded. He shed his Western clothes in favor of a loincloth, of course. But he continued to wear tennis shoes—his feet had grown soft in the city.

Worse, especially in the eyes of his tribal contemporaries, Waysersera could no longer fish with agility or keep up on the trail. His work with the spear was clumsy and inaccurate, and he had lost the stamina he needed to compete in races. His friends teased him without mercy.

It was quite a blow for a young man used to popularity and praise. The tribal elders made comments such as, "What good is a Barí who acquires the tools of modern society but is no longer capable of shooting a turkey or spearing a fish?" He had lost respect within the tribe.

One day Waysersera shared his problems with me. His frustration boiled over; he was in tears. This was highly unusual, as Motilones are taught to keep such feelings under control.

According to the Motilone tradition,
a medicine man or woman must
determine the "real" reason for a
child's death. He weighs any previous
negative actions by the parents,
as well as taboos believed to be
cast on them.

For his sake, I felt my response needed to echo that of any other tribal elder. "Waysersera, you mustn't let your emotions get the best of you. You must make them work for you instead. Channel them for greater strength and focus in your running and hunting and fishing."

Waysersera accepted my challenge. He worked hard at renewing his skills and began having some success. By the end of his school break he had recaptured his past abilities and was again regarded with favor by the rest of the tribe.

Waysersera's determination paid off in other ways as well. When Kaymiyokba was named president of the newly formed Motilone-Barí Association in 1979, Waysersera was chosen as vice president. In 1984, while in law school, he received an even greater honor. Colombia's minister of government announced that Waysersera would fill the newly created position of secretary of Indian affairs. He became the first Motilone to hold a government cabinet position.

Daniel Adjibacbayra was the youngest member of our group. An orphan like Kaymiyokba, Adjibacbayra took an interest in me when he was about seven years old. He followed me around during the day in Iquiacarora, and I used to feed him and make sure he was taken care of.

When he was thirteen, Adjibacbayra developed a severe case of cirrhosis of the liver. He wasted away to little more than skin and bones. I arranged for him to be admitted to a hospital in Bogotá, where doctors removed three-quarters of his liver. After the surgery, he was unconscious for a month and a half. He was not expected to live. But we prayed for Adjibacbayra and anointed him with oil. Through the skill of the physicians and the faith of his people, he recovered.

After his brush with death, Adjibacbayra grew into a stocky, powerful young man. He was no taller than Waysersera but had the strength to carry a large animal through the jungle for two days.

Adjibacbayra was an excellent student in the jungle schools. He learned to speak perfect Spanish and was perhaps the best organizer of all the Motilones. Later, he also became president of the Motilone-Barí Community of Colombia Association. He was in office when the Colombian government budgeted funds for Motilone-Barí Association programs for the first time. In the frequently corrupt government system in Colombia, when monies are sent to groups such as the Motilone-Barí Association, the government officials who provided the funds expected a "kickback." Adjibacbayra refused to send the kickback, setting a precedent that all allocated funds would be used for the benefit of the tribes.

Waysersera could no longer fish
with agility or keep up on the trail.
His work with the spear was clumsy and
inaccurate, and he had lost the stamina
he needed to compete in races.

These four colleagues of mine, and many more, had taken full advantage of the educational opportunities now available to the Motilones. Not all who pursued these new avenues were men. By 1985, for example, Patricia, Brigit, and Patrocinia Undachira had completed studies in family hygiene and preventive medicine at the Institute of Ocana. And Bobby's daughter Cuadudura was one of several Motilones enrolled in the Advanced State School of Pedagogy in Bucaramanga.

I did not view education as the goal. Rather, it was a tool to equip men and women with the ability to navigate their future. And it would only reach its full potential if combined with the wisdom of heaven, such as in the example set by Bobaríshora. As Cuadudura said, "I shall serve my people with my best refined talents, just as my father did. I shall always walk as my father—on the path of life, in the steps of Jesus Christ."

At the Third Congress of Frontier Policies, the Motilone delegation described these achievements in education and other programs, and the government representatives listened. I believe it did lead to a greater openness and interest among Colombia's leaders in integrating the nation's indigenous populations into the rest of society.

The Motilone delegation was responsible for several key political victories. First, the governments of Colombia and Venezuela now recognize Motilones as internationally privileged inhabitants of the frontiers. This means that they are allowed to travel throughout their native Motilone territory—which is comprised of land in both Colombia and Venezuela—and they may cross the borders of the two countries without confrontation.

Second, the Colombian government respects the traditional values and independence of the Motilones. The Colombian government even appointed Dacsarara, the Motilone whose eloquence before the congress convinced them to grant the Motilones their territory, as the country's director of Indian affairs.

The governments of Colombia and
Venezuela now recognize Motilones
as internationally privileged inhabitants
of the frontiers. They are allowed to travel
throughout their native territory and
cross the borders of the two countries
without confrontation.

Third, the Indians have been given protection for their lands. This is very crucial in light of the current drug trafficking crisis and the brutal conflicts between right-wing paramilitary groups and left-wing guerrilla rebel forces. Some indigenous tribes are nearing extinction as a result of the clash between these violent factions. Indigenous people need protection from violence, exploitation, and displacement by illegal armed groups, and the Motilones have made great strides in securing this type of protection for themselves and other Indian tribes.

Fourth, both countries' governments provide financial help to the indigenous communities for acceptable goals in development. This help includes scholarships and loans for the continuance of the Motilones' education. But to keep the Indians from becoming beggars, a revolving funds program was established. This is a program where one group of Motilones raises a herd of cattle and gives the offspring to another group. The second group then raises that herd of cattle and gives the offspring to another group, and so on. Each group can then sell the cattle and use the money to fund their development needs, including paying for scholarships and government loans for education.

Colombia's national newspapers also recognized the significance of Motilone participation in developing strong relationships with people isolated in the frontier. Surprisingly, they acknowledged the spiritual impact that the Motilones brought to these discussions as well. One reporter wrote, "The Motilones injected new vitality and hope in the light of past failures of supposedly brilliant programs. The Motilones are practical and dedicated to goals beyond the physical limits. They have a spiritual enlightenment beyond our grasp."

Chapter 9

The Motilone Miracle

Have the outsiders intruded further on our lands since they joined the co-ops? No. By working with us, they have learned to understand and respect us.

—BOBARÍSHORA

The sustained success of the Motilone programs in education, medicine, and agriculture might never have taken place if not for the cooperatives. I am not a socialist, nor for that matter do I consider myself a capitalist. At the time—the late 1960s—I was simply looking for an economic enterprise that might best allow the Motilones to become self-sufficient and to acquire the tools they needed without resorting to ambushing outsiders. I was familiar with cooperatives because of my father's work in Minnesota, and I was able to extract more information from his contacts in Venezuela.

I saw the cooperatives as the key to a five-point plan for community development among the Motilones. First, we would try to prevent the disastrous effects of epidemics that resulted from contact with outsiders through inoculations and increased use of preventative medical procedures. Second, we would improve the health of the Indians through a greater variety in diet. This would be accomplished by introducing crops to the jungle—corn, beans, rice, and more—and later, cattle. This would also be a step in helping the tribes improve their quality of life.

The third point—negotiating with the national governments to secure legal protections for traditional Motilone territories—was critical in order to preserve the Motilones' access to land and water. This effort was crowned with success in 1974 when President Misael Pastrana signed legislation that recognized Motilone territories.

When the Motilones realized the power of the written word, it awakened a thirst for education—the fourth point. We would establish schools so that the Motilones would learn how to read and write. This allowed them to read God's Word for themselves as we completed translations of Scripture and enabled them to communicate with Western society on its own terms.

The final point, the one that would fund and provide a foundation for all the others, was the establishment of a cooperative system. Christ said, "If you have faith as small as a mustard seed...nothing will be impossible for you" (Matt. 17:20–21). Instead of a mustard seed, we would put our faith in a cocoa bean.

It was in some ways an unlikely road to success. The Motilones had no experience with harvesting any crop, let alone chocolate. But I felt it was the logical thing to do. It also fostered an environment of cooperation and respect for others, which seemed in keeping with what they were learning about the ways of Christ.

In the beginning, we determined that 40 percent of cooperative profits would be dedicated to social work—half to Motilone schools and half to the health centers. The rest would be set aside as capital for the cooperatives. It was slow going at first. We made very little money. Step by step, however, our profit margin improved. Eventually the Motilones were able to dedicate 60 percent of profits toward social needs.

These programs were gradually accepted by the tribes as they observed the benefits that resulted. Yet there was resistance, particularly to the concept of cooperatives. The younger, more progressive leaders in the tribe, such as Bobby, saw the potential of the co-op model and were willing to give it a try. But many of the elders had no use for the idea, especially when the others voted to allow some land settlers to participate.

One of these elders was Bobby's father-in-law, Aberdora. Then about sixty, Aberdora was an aggressive and respected warrior who had wounded or killed a number of outsiders. He was proud of the "trophies" he'd won in battle—a six-foot metal measuring rod that he'd sharpened into a spear; a necklace that included buttons from the shirts of his victims. He wore an oil company safety helmet so often that the lining wore out and left him with a bald spot above his forehead.

> We determined that 40 percent of cooperative profits would be dedicated to social work—half to Motilone schools and half to the health centers. The rest would be set aside as capital for the cooperatives.

This assertive chieftain watched with disdain as colonists were allowed safe passage into the jungle to trade tools for investment in the cooperative.

"These are our enemies!" he would say to other Motilones. "They bring sickness. They want to destroy our jungle. They shoot animals in the trees with their firing sticks and make them disappear. Why do we want them close to us?"

Aberdora continued to observe and argue. But as he watched the colonists and co-ops, he also noticed a change in his daughter, Atacadara, after she married Bobaríshora and allowed Saymaydodji-ibateradacura into her heart. She was more joyful, more peaceful. He also saw the kind of man and husband that Bobaríshora had become. It piqued his curiosity. He began to investigate this leader named "Jesus Christ" and what He stood for. He remained curious during a two-year bout with tuberculosis, from which he finally recovered.

Still, he remained opposed to the co-ops.

I remember that final argument with Bobby. It was early evening, and a chorus of katydids chirped near the longhouse. Bobby and some of the other co-op members had just returned from an afternoon of collecting chocolate beans and had collapsed, exhausted, into their hammocks. Aberdora, wearing his safety helmet, sauntered over and launched into one of his typical offensives against the co-ops and the colonists.

"You will have to wait a very long time for your chocolate to grow into something you can trade for a machete," he said to Bobby and the others. "You are not being practical. And in the meantime, what will be our policy against these intruders from civilization? They are not good for us. We must shoot them with arrows."

"Yes, you can shoot them," Bobby said in a tone that betrayed exasperation. "But what would have happened if you shot the people who brought the pills that cured your tuberculosis? You would be dead. Not only you, but also two hundred other Barí."

Aberdora opened his mouth to respond, then stopped. It was unusual for his son-in-law to speak so forcefully to him. But he had a point. Aberdora hadn't considered where the medicine had come from.

Bobby pressed his advantage. "Where would our tribe be without the chocolate profits that allow us to purchase our medicines? Where would we be if we could not purchase materials for our schools?"

Aberdora had learned to read and write in the school at Iquiacarora. He had enjoyed showing everyone the day he learned to write his own name.

"Have the outsiders intruded further on our lands since they joined the co-ops?" Bobby continued. "No. By working with us, they have learned to understand and respect us. The co-ops are good policy for us."

Aberdora was silent for several seconds. "It is a good argument," he said finally. "I will think about these words."

Bobby was encouraged. For his father-in-law to concede anything during a disagreement was a victory in itself.

Aberdora did contemplate Bobby's words. He spent even more time observing the operation of the co-cops, and he actually met some of the colonists. He discovered that they weren't as terrible or different as he thought. They had their own problems to deal with.

Eventually, Aberdora concluded that the cooperatives *were* beneficial to his people. It wasn't too long after that he joined the board of directors of the Motilone-Barí Cooperative, its official name under Colombian law. But that was not the biggest change in his heart. Like so many of his fellow Motilones, he also made the decision to walk on the trail of Jesus.

The Motilones were not the only people with reservations about their new neighbors. There was resistance and prejudice on the side of the colonists as well.

One of these land settlers was a man named Don Jorge. The father of six children, Jorge was known to be antagonistic toward the Indians. He felt the Motilones had no claim to any of the jungle lands. We heard that he made comments such as, "The Indians are useless and lazy," and, "Wherever there are Indians, there are always problems."

Jorge had problems of his own. I learned later that he was having difficulty paying back a loan; he was also estranged from his wife.

One day, several of the Motilones had gathered in the longhouse when we heard the news: Don Jorge was dead. He had ended his own life.

A discussion ensued about whether the Motilones should respond. Some were just pleased to be rid of a troublemaker. But others, including Arabadoyca and Kaymiyokba, argued that the tribe should share some of the co-op food surplus. It was an opportunity to demonstrate the compassion of Saymaydodji-ibateradacura.

"The head of the family is gone and the family is suffering," Kaymiyokba said. "The mother has several children. What are they going to do?"

The Indians asked for my opinion. "I think it is a good idea to share with them," I said. "It's a way of showing your concern for people outside your community. This is one of the reasons we established the cooperatives, to help with social needs."

"Yes," said one Motilone, "but if someone else dies, are we going to give food to them, too?"

"Well, perhaps by God's grace, yes," I said. "But if you have a different revelation from God, then no. I would respect your decision either way."

The cooperative directors decided to give a box of surplus food to Don Jorge's family. The next month, they sent another box. This continued for two years.

Jorge's widow was overwhelmed. She couldn't believe that the Indians her husband had so consistently maligned would be generous with her.

I thought this gesture was merely another example of the Motilones' growing maturity in Christ. It was not until many years later that I discovered a hidden, long-term effect—one that would save my life.

By 1986, the government recognized both the Motilone-Barí Cooperative, at the junction of Caño Tomas River and the Rio de Oro, and the AsocBarí Trading Post, on the Catatumbo River, as legally registered cooperatives. The trading post opened two additional co-op centers, which covered nearly the entire area populated by the Motilones. The AsocBarí Trading Post counted more than three hundred members, including many land settlers.

What was most fulfilling to me, however, was watching the Motilones use the cooperatives as a means to emulate the example of Christ. By this time they were providing nurses for six non-Motilone Indian tribes. They were sharing cattle with the Yuko, Huamonae, Cogi, Tunebo, and Pijau Indians, retaining only enough for their minimum needs.

The Motilones helped the Huamonae construct a community riverboat and equipped them with a motor. Motilone law students provided technical assistance

I thought this gesture was merely another example of the Motilones' growing maturity in Christ. It was not until many years later that I discovered a hidden, long-term effect—one that would save my life.

for organizing and obtaining legal status for the new Huamonae Association. The Motilones also built a residence to lodge chronically ill patients in the Eastern Plains region.

Perhaps the greatest example of Motilone "outreach" at this time came in late 1985 and 1986 after the eruption of Nevado del Ruiz in the state of Tolima, about fifty miles west of Bogotá. I had helped organize a sugar cooperative for the Pijau Indians in Tolima about three years earlier, and a number of the Motilones were involved in explaining the gospel message to the Pijau.

In the late afternoon of November 13, 1985, pumice fragments and ash fell from the sky onto Amero, a town of 27,000 people at the base of Nevado del Ruiz and adjacent to Pijau Indian territory. It was the initial blast from the volcano. The citizens of Amero and the Indians remained calm, however. They had experienced minor earthquakes and steam explosions for nearly a year, so this was not so out of the ordinary.

Because of the ash, the Red Cross ordered an evacuation of Amero at 7:00 p.m., but the ash stopped falling a few minutes later and the evacuation was called off.

Just after 9:00 p.m., molten rock erupted from the summit crater of Nevado del Ruiz—but storm clouds blocked any view from below of the explosion. Less than two hours later, an enormous wave of mud, water, and hot volcanic debris roared over Amero and the rest of the countryside. The citizens and the Indians hadn't seen it coming and had no chance to escape. Three quarters of the residents of Amero were drowned or buried alive, as well as hundreds of Pijau Indians. In all, more than 23,000 people were killed. It was the second-deadliest volcanic event of the twentieth century.

Besides the Pijau who perished, others were injured, homes were lost, and land destroyed. The Colombian government and charitable foundations responded to the needs of the remaining townspeople in the region, but there was no help for the Pijau Indians hidden in the mountain valleys. In the aftermath of the tragedy, however, the spiritual connection between the Pijau and the Motilones remained.

The Motilones took action. I was part of a team that spent the rest of 1985 with the Pijau. We sent six nurses and allocated funds for medicine, clothing, basic kitchen utensils, blankets, food, and relocation of the victims. The Motilones spent nearly $10,000 on disaster relief for their native brethren.

All of these activities on behalf of indigenous peoples of Colombia were made possible, either partly or completely, by the resources of the cooperatives. What had begun as an abstract concept—a program of community development for the Indians founded on something as simple as a cocoa bean—had become reality.

The Motilones were not dependent only on their dwindling hunting grounds for survival. Nor did they need to beg for handouts from the government or benevolent organizations. Instead, they had achieved an unprecedented level of financial independence.

I have often marveled at what has taken place. Though I presented a plan that was completely unfamiliar to the Motilones, they had a simple and abiding belief that it was part of God's work in their lives. Their faith was perhaps only as large as a mustard seed—or a cocoa bean—yet it was more than enough. I praised Him for what some in the media had begun calling "The Motilone Miracle."

I was soon to discover that He had even more miracles in mind.

Bruchko and the Motilone Miracle

The Stone Age scene when Bruce arrived in ▲ the early 1960s.

Bruce hunting with Motilones in ▲ the jungle.

Bruce talking with a ▶ Motilone in his early days among them.

◀ Bruce smiles for the camera with the river and jungle scenery in the background.

Arabadoyca and children watch Bruce taste some Motilone cooking. ▼

Bobaríshora, ▲
"Bobby," draws his
bow while hunting in
the jungle clearing.

Bruce with Bobaríshora, ▶
"Bobby," the first
Motilone to receive
Christ.

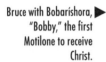

Bobaríshora, "Bobby," leads a group of Motilones
on a 1966 canoe excursion. ▼

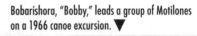

Olson, with a native child, during his ▲
early days in the jungle.

Bruce (holding monkey) ▲
and Bobaríshora, "Bobby,"
visit the United States.

◀ Bobaríshora (right) displays a weapon
during a meeting in the United States.

Olson (far right) defends the rights of the Motilones
at the Organization of American States. ▼

Motilone children enjoy life in the jungle.

Piggy back.

Motilone children
playing in the river. ▼

▲ A brother and sister in the river.

A young girl peeks through
the thatched leaves used
for longhouse construction. ▼

▲ A Motilone girl weaves a basket.

◀ A Motilone mother hugs her child.

▲ A Motilone woman weaving a basket.

◀ A woman cares for her children on a mat inside the longhouse.

A woman cleans ▶ frogs for her family's next meal.

A typical day inside the longhouse.

◀ A Motilone dropping rocks in the river to form the fishing dam.

▲ A man ready to catch fish with his spear.

▲ A Motilone fishing in the river.

▲ A Motilone boy carries bijau leaves to help the men build the dam.

Motilone men add the final touch to their fishing dam. ▼

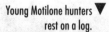
Motilone hunters on the trail at night.

Young Motilone hunters rest on a log.

Cleaning a fresh catch of fish. ▲

▲ Hunters make their own arrows and customize them with identifying marks.

A Motilone uses light from the doorway of the longhouse to make an arrow. ▶

Constructing a longhouse.

Headlines tell of Bruce's captivity and call for his safe release.

▲ Bruce featured in Colombian comic strip.

GOOD NEWS ! BRUCE IS ALIVE!
·THANK'S GOD!

APRIL 1 DE 1989
I, BRUCE OLSSON POLITICAL PRISONER OF THE GUERRILLA FRONT "ARMANDO CACUA" ADSCRIPT TO THE WAR FRONT OF THE NORTEAST ARMY OF NATIONAL LIBERATION OF COLOMBIA INFORM TO ALL THOSE INTERESTED THAT ACTUALLY I AM IN PERFECT CONDITIONS IN THE CAMP OF THE NEW COLOMBIA.
BRUCE OLSSON

This picture of Bruce was sent to our community with his hand writing letter .(We include a fragment and translation of it) He is alive and well.

What a good Fortune ! we are full of happiness! God bless him!. we now need more of your prayers and financial support to continue with Bruce's projects.

He will come back and know that we have done well during his absence because we all have learn from his good examples and also have had God's guidance all the way.

In the name of the Lord.
Thanks you very much . God bless you all
Jorge and Motion Bari Council
Please write:Jorge Kaymiyokba
Apartado Aereo 40008
Bucaramanga . Colombia S.A.

The Motilones spread the word about Bruce's captivity after receiving ▲ a handwritten note and photograph to prove he is still alive.

Bruce surrounded by the Motilones. ◀

▲ Julio's self-portrait "A Poor Reflection" wins "Best Photograph 2001."

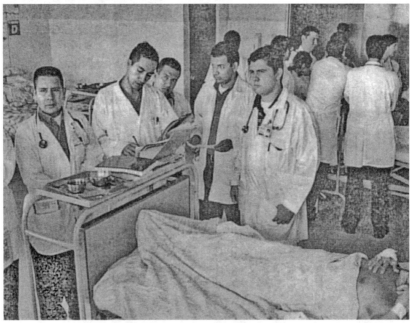

▲ David Tegria Uncaria (far left) is the eighth medical physician to graduate under Bruce's sponsorship.

Chapter 10

Increasing Danger

God, we ask You today to spare our brother Yado. We claim Your healing power for him as promised in Your holy words to us.

—KAYMIYOKBA

The jungles of South America are full of natural dangers that threaten even the most experienced native. For a bibliophile from Minnesota who grew up with no interest in the Boy Scouts or the great outdoors, they offer what sometimes feels like one perilous adventure after another.

Among the most deadly representatives of the Colombian-Venezuelan jungle's animal kingdom are panthers, jaguars, and crocodiles. But the most prevalent are an inordinate variety of snakes. Rattlesnakes. Coral snakes. Water moccasins that carry a potent poison in their venom. Boa constrictors that grow up to ten feet in length and prefer to squeeze their victims to death. And the largest of them all, the anaconda, which has been measured at up to thirty-seven feet, although it is believed that even longer anacondas live in the unexplored areas of the South American jungles. Though such incidents are rare, the anaconda has been known to swallow a man whole.

By staying alert while walking on the trail it is usually possible to spot and avoid the most dangerous signs of trouble. But it is impossible to stay alert at every moment, or to anticipate every potential source of danger.

I recall one incident when I was traveling alone. I'd been on foot for two days and was exhausted. It was the wet season, so I had brought a malleable sheet of plastic to wrap around myself at night. That evening, after carefully checking the ground for bugs and nests, I slipped into my plastic cocoon and drifted off to sleep. The night was humid, however. I tossed and turned in my makeshift bed. At one point I must have thrown the plastic off.

I woke up on my back about four in the morning, feeling uncomfortable. Slivers of moonlight slanted through the trees over me. I listened to the sounds of the jungle—clicking beetles, a gentle breeze. Somewhere in the distance an owl hooted. Nothing seemed amiss.

Then I felt something leathery shift against my chest. My senses snapped to full attention.

Gently, I lifted my head a few inches. As my body moved almost imperceptibly, I detected the same leathery sensation not only on my chest but also along both sides of my body. I peered down. In the darkness, I could make out not one—not even two—but three large snakes pressed against me.

I shivered and tried not to breathe.

I couldn't tell what type of snake they were, but I had to assume they were poisonous—probably 80 percent of South American jungle snakes are deadly. Yet these three had made no move to harm me. Most likely, during the cool of the night, they had simply discovered a warm place to snuggle up for a rest.

And so I settled in to wait. For more than an hour, I shared my space on the jungle floor with three of God's least popular creatures, taking all precautions to avoid sneezing! Finally, the sun rose and the temperature increased. The snakes no longer required my body heat. One by one, they slithered away and out of sight.

I stood and stretched. It felt wonderful. This was not the most relaxing way to begin a day, but God had given me another one, and I was grateful.

Then there was the time when I was traveling in the jungle with a group of Motilones. We had all bedded down for the evening. I was extremely hungry—we'd had very little to eat. But I dozed off quickly.

Early the next morning I was still asleep, having the most interesting dream. A large, blue butterfly was in my mouth. I liked the butterfly, but decided it was time to let him go. I opened my mouth, but the butterfly did not leave.

I began to wake up, though I was still groggy. Was there a butterfly in my mouth? I reached in with my thumb and first finger. Something *was* there! I grabbed hold and pulled…and kept pulling.

To my horror, a brown roundworm—at least a foot in length—emerged from my mouth. It seemed I wasn't the only hungry creature that night! The roundworm, an intestinal parasite, had crawled up my esophagus while I slept, apparently looking for something to eat after finding my digestive system empty.

I gagged and tossed the roundworm away, then gagged some more, stomping about our makeshift campsite and creating quite a scene.

A few of the Motilones were already awake and had witnessed my "magician's trick." It must have been more entertaining for them than it was for me. I thought they would never stop giggling.

For more than an hour, I shared
my space on the jungle floor with three
of God's least popular creatures, taking
all precautions to avoid sneezing!

Less amusing was my trek with Kaymiyokba and a Motilone named Axjuanira. It was late 1987, and we were walking through the jungle near the headwaters of the Rio de Oro. We had already been on the trail for four days. I was so fatigued I could barely walk in a straight line.

We stopped to rest. I saw a large pile of brown and green leaves and thought, *It would be so nice to just plop down in that pile of leaves.* Even in my addled state of mind, I realized that would be dangerous. What I should have done was test the area with a long stick. Instead, too tired to search for a testing instrument, I used my right leg to disturb the pile. It was not a wise decision.

It took only a moment for the creature hidden beneath the leaves to strike. I saw the flash of movement and yanked my leg back, but it was too late. I felt a sharp pain just above my ankle. I recognized my attacker as a bushmaster snake, identifiable by its tan coloring and the large diamond shapes along its back. The bushmaster is the largest venomous snake in the world. This one was four feet long.

I'd already been bitten by poisonous snakes twice before and had survived by administering an antidote. But doctors had told me that my body wouldn't handle a third dose of the serum—the antidote itself would kill me.

And so, because of my own carelessness, I was in mortal danger. The looks on the faces of Kaymiyokba and Axjuanira reflected their concern. I heard Axjuanira whisper, "Look at that wound. He can't survive that. He's going to die."

It would be an understatement to say that the effects of poisonous snakebites are most unpleasant. The first symptoms are dizziness about five minutes after the attack. Internal hemorrhaging will follow. The victim may bleed from the eyes and nose within an hour. Death comes in another twenty-four to forty-eight hours.

I sat down on the trail to wait. There was nothing else to do.

I felt a sharp pain just above my ankle. I recognized my attacker as a bushmaster snake.

Kaymiyokba and I had recently finished a Barí translation of the Book of James, which included the passage, "Is any one of you sick? He should call the elders of the church to pray over him and anoint him with oil in the name of the Lord. And the prayer offered in faith will make the sick person well; the Lord will raise him up" (James 5:14–15).

Now Kaymiyokba reached into his backpack and produced a small bottle of olive oil. Soberly, he sprinkled this over my head. Then he and Axjuanira placed their hands on my shoulders.

"God, we ask You today to spare our brother Yado," he prayed. "We claim your healing power for him as promised in Your holy words to us. Heal him from this snake wound. Return him to us in full health in the name of Saymaydodji-ibateradacura."

I was moved by this simple and sincere prayer by my friends. I felt that I had perfect peace with God, that I was where I was supposed to be. My mind quieted and my spirit grew serene.

Though I was prepared for it, the dizziness did not come. A few minutes later, still feeling no ill effects, I got up, and we continued on our journey.

A skeptic will say that the snake didn't inject any poison—that it had expelled its venom recently or that it was only protecting its territory and withheld its deadly toxin. This may be true. But what God's Spirit wrote on my heart that day is that my life is continuously in His hands. My homecoming will be at His election—not a second before, and not a moment after. It is a reassuring thought.

In case I forget the lesson, I still have the fang marks on my leg as a reminder.

Panthers and snakes are dangerous, but at least they are visible threats. More insidious are diseases that can strike without the victim ever knowing it.

Since they have no natural immunity built up, the Motilones are particularly vulnerable to diseases such as tuberculosis and measles that are carried to the jungle by outsiders. An outbreak of measles in 1966, for example, killed many Motilones. I myself have battled malaria, hepatitis, and typhoid fever in the jungle. The latter once left me weak and useless for three months. My most persistent difficulty, however, has been Chagas' disease. It is transmitted to humans by triatomine insects, sometimes called "kissing bugs" because they prefer to bite humans around the mouth and eyes while they are sleeping. I was infected in the 1960s during a visit to Venezuela's Orinoco region and was ill for months.

There is no cure for Chagas' disease, though some medications help to relieve symptoms. It often lies dormant for years, as it did with me, before returning with even greater strength. My symptoms have included muscle aches and fever, and more recently, chest pains and infrequent periods when I am almost paralyzed for a day or two. I have undergone three eye surgeries due to complications of the disease.

I have heard of experimental techniques that show promise in treating Chagas' disease and hope that these will someday prove effective for those of us who are infected.

A person gets used to living with danger, whether it is traveling on foot through a South American jungle or traveling on a concrete highway while surrounded by metal machines hurtling at high speed. But neither of these compare to the danger that confronted all of us in the Colombian jungles in the late 1980s—and continues to this day.

There are four major armed opposition groups known by their Spanish initials—the Revolutionary Armed Forces of Colombia (FARC), the National Liberation Army (ELN), Maoist People's Liberation Army (EPL), and Movement of April 19 (M19). These rebel groups, along with the paramilitary allies of the government, are responsible for the current human rights crisis in Colombia, which now leads the world in kidnappings and where it is estimated that one person is murdered every fifteen minutes and hundreds of thousands more are displaced each year.[1]

For a number of years, these violent left-wing revolutionary organizations had been increasingly active throughout the nation's rural areas. By the late 1980s, they were encroaching on Motilone territory. Most of the land settlers in our area were in support of the guerrillas. Those who were not, including many of the Christian colonists, either fled to the cities or were killed.

I was not unsympathetic to the cause of the insurgents. They were born with idealistic intentions in the sixties and seventies out of the frequently corrupt and oppressive practices of the wealthy and of the Colombian government. I did not blame people for wanting to do something about the appalling conditions in which they lived. Yet I knew that threats, kidnappings, and murders would never be the answer.

> I did not blame people for wanting to do
> something about the appalling conditions
> in which they lived. Yet I knew that
> threats, kidnappings, and murders
> would never be the answer.

In 1985, members of M19 took two hundred hostages and seized the Palace of Justice in Bogotá. A day later, after a fierce battle, more than one hundred security forces, civilians, and guerrillas lay dead. It was just one example of the extreme measures the revolutionaries were willing to take.

On another occasion, the ELN kidnapped a pilot who was to coordinate air services for medical commitments we had made to tribal peoples in Colombia's southeastern plains. In the same month, four land settlers and two government soldiers were killed during combat with guerrillas.

Opposing the revolutionaries was the military arm of the government, as well as right-wing paramilitary forces that sympathized with the existing government but operated outside the law. Complicating the situation further was another growing presence—the drug cartels. Many of the guerrillas and their leaders had abandoned their initial allegiances as a people's movement and formed alliances with the cartels. Perhaps some felt it was only a temporary solution to their funding problems. But the enormous dollars and power available through trafficking of cocaine, produced with Western-made chemicals and sold primarily to the West, quickly corrupted even the most idealistic guerrillas. Some estimate the value of Colombia's drug cartel shipments to the United States since 1990 to be as high as $10 billion.[2]

The Motilones and I tried to maintain a position of neutrality regarding the violent factions surrounding us. But the guerrillas coveted Motilone land, both as a training ground for recruits and as an ideal place to grow cocaine without government interference. They also began stealing funds from the co-ops, which devastated our operation.

Since I had rejected previous attempts to recruit me into the guerrilla movements, I myself had received three warnings to leave the country or be eliminated. Though concerned, I felt secure. I trusted in God's sovereignty and my position of unity with the Motilones.

Then, in the early months of 1988, I was summoned to Bogotá by Colombia's minister of national defense, who supported my presence in the jungle. He and I had spoken before about my status and security in Colombia. Though many in the government regarded me sympathetically for my work with the Motilones, others mistrusted my motives and influence. I had become a controversial figure. At the minister's invitation, I had recently become a naturalized citizen of Colombia. It helped removed doubts about my intentions and commitment to the nation's indigenous peoples. It also reflected the pride I felt about my place in Colombia.

Now, however, the minister emphasized the seriousness of my situation. Guerrillas captured by the Colombian military had revealed that I was considered a military target.

For the first time, I felt threatened by the circumstances closing in. At this point I traveled almost exclusively at night. I did not intend to be reckless with my safety. I knew the difference between presumption and faith. I would not tempt God, but I would continue my ministry with the Motilones and fourteen neighboring tribal peoples while trusting in Him for guidance and protection.

I wrote in a note to two of my American supporters, "It is sad, this unrest. Man is truly able to complicate life. Man is appointed to rule yet is so often overruled by circumstances, inner and outer ones. May the Lord help us all to be true peacemakers in the situation—not arising anger but rather awakening a deeper awareness of and respect for the true dignity of humanity."

It was not much later that Kaymiyokba and I decided to risk the daytime trip to the cooperative at Saphadana. October 24, 1988, was a picturesque day in the land some call "Motilonia." Sunlight reflected off the aqua-tinged waters of the Rio de Oro, the River of Gold, as a gentle breeze blew in the same direction as the current. It was hard to imagine that we could be in any danger in such a setting.

Events quickly proved just how wrong I was. The two guerrillas on the beach. Machine-gun fire. The startling announcement that I was to become a prisoner. The rifle barrel in my mouth. The rush of memories.

And the wondering... would this be the moment I go home to God?

Chapter 11

Captivity

I have come to stop the disease inside you. I come to give you warmth.
—CHIGBARÍ, GOD'S MOTILONE MESSENGER

To my surprise, the guerrilla hovering over me with the rifle didn't pull the trigger. Instead, he grabbed my arm and yanked me to my feet. About thirty guerrillas closed in. One tied my hands behind me.

The rifle jabbed me in the back toward the jungle. It was time to march. I caught a last glimpse of my friends on the beach, still covered by a pair of guerrillas with machine guns. Kaymiyokba and the rest were watching closely but making no further moves to resist. *Good*, I thought. *Perhaps they will escape safely.*

We quickly disappeared beneath the jungle canopy. We marched without rest until evening, when we stopped at the home of a colonist who was apparently in league with the guerrillas. I was given a cup of broth, but by then my fever from the malaria was so high that I couldn't eat anything. Later, my fever finally broke. A woman, the mother of the colonist who lived there, approached. "Olson, can I get you anything?" she said. "You do not look well." This time I was able to sip some broth.

About midnight I was pulled to my feet for another march. On foot and later by canoe, we traveled deeper and deeper into the jungle over the next three days. Finally we reached the makeshift camp where I was to remain for the following two weeks. I had been told that I was only being detained because the leader of the movement wanted to speak to me, and that I would soon be released. But it quickly became obvious that this was a lie. There would be no early release. The guerrillas had been ordered to capture me and await further instructions.

It was the wet season, and the rains were relentless. A makeshift shelter was constructed over my hammock at the camp, but it offered virtually no protection from the elements. I was always soaking wet, even when the rain let up for a few hours, as it did on rare occasions. Even with the sun out, it was so humid that my shoes and clothes never dried.

Over time, I developed the patience to see
and hear God in the subscripts of life. And
I learned from experience that even when
I couldn't sense what He was doing, I could
trust that He was always there, always
working out His sovereign will.

Despite the circumstances, I was able to keep my spirits up. People often ask me if I ever blamed God for my predicament, but that was the furthest thing from my mind. While I obviously hoped to be rescued, I also believed it was my responsibility to serve Him right where I was. What I asked of God each day was simple and practical: *Father, I'm alive, and I want to use this time constructively. How can I be useful to You today?* I knew that He, not my captors, was in control.

I had awakened to the fullness of His sovereignty many years before during a Motilone hunting expedition. Our intrusion into the jungle that day brought the usual reaction from assorted birds and monkeys, but as we quietly slipped through the dense undergrowth I noticed a sudden escalation in the volume and intensity of the cacophony. Thousands of katydids joined the animal squawks and screeches, raising the noise level to the point where our human voices were drowned out. I had never heard anything like it.

Astonished, I shouted to the Motilone ahead of me on the trail, "Listen to that! Isn't it incredible?"

He nodded. "Yes," he called back. "We heard it, too. It's a piping turkey!"

His remark stopped me in my tracks. A piping turkey? All I had heard was chaotic, ear-shattering racket! How could anyone notice the voice of one lone turkey in the midst of this din?

My companion saw my confusion and signaled me to stop and listen. It was several minutes before I began to pick out which sounds were which—animals, birds, insects, humans. Then, slowly, the separate voices became more distinct. Finally, after more patient listening, I heard it. Behind the hue and cry of the jungle, behind the voices of my companions, behind the quiet sound of my own breathing, was the haunting, reedy voice of the piping turkey, calling out as if it were inside a hollow tube.

It was a poignant moment for me. I wondered what else I'd missed—not only in the jungle, but also in my own spiritual life. How much had I overlooked when I'd failed to patiently tune in to God's subtle voice in the midst of life's chaos and stresses?

In the years that followed, the piping turkey often came to mind when I struggled to discern God's voice and sense His quiet presence during perplexing or discouraging situations. Over time, I developed the patience to see and hear God in the subscripts of life. And I learned from experience that even when I couldn't sense what He was doing, I could trust that He was always there, always working out His sovereign will, even when I was too overwhelmed by the "noise" to notice or appreciate His complex orchestrations.

As the days in the guerrilla camp wore on, it became more and more important for me to remember that God had a purpose for my abduction. Having my freedom taken away from me was difficult to accept. But God had never let me down. I had to trust Him here—hidden in the jungle as a hostage of armed rebels—just as before.

Or maybe more than ever.

One day, about a month after my abduction and after we had shifted between several camps, four guerrillas approached me. They all wore camouflage; two carried rifles. I recognized one of the unarmed ones, a short man in his late twenties wearing a red beret, as the leader of the contingent that had captured me. I had learned that his name was Alejandro. He directed one of the others to untie my hands.

Alejandro handed me a pad of paper and a pen. He spoke in crisp Spanish: "Olson, you will write letters to the chiefs of the Motilone Indians. Tell them that the ELN wishes to begin a peaceful dialogue with them. Tell them that you are well and that you believe it is wise for them to consider incorporating with us."

So here it was, finally. The guerrillas wanted me to use my influence with the Motilones to manipulate them into an agreement: free passage and use of Motilone territory in exchange for peace and, presumably, my release.

Without a word, I scribbled out a statement in Barí, explaining where I was in the jungle and the situation I was in and advising my friends to assess the area with great caution. I handed the note to Alejandro.

"This is no good," he said after looking at it. "We don't want you to write in the Indian language. You must write in Spanish." He handed me the pad again.

This time I wrote that I was alive and well as a prisoner of the revolutionaries. The guerrilla leader read my message. (See a copy of the letter and photograph in the photo section.)

As I entered what I estimated to be
the fourth month of my confinement
to the palm tree, I moved closer to the
edge of reality. I was terribly lonely.

"This says nothing about beginning a dialogue. You must write more."

"No," I said. "I am happy to communicate with the Motilones, but I will not encourage them to begin a dialogue with the ELN or any of the guerrilla movements. That is a decision only they can make."

Alejandro stared at me. A macaw screeched in the distance. One of the guerrillas coughed.

"You must write this," Alejandro said, his eyes boring into mine. "If you do not... you will regret your position."

I shook my head.

Alejandro's face turned red. He spoke to an associate, who left for a few minutes, then returned carrying a chain about two yards long. Alejandro grabbed the rifle held by one of the guerrillas standing next to him. He pointed it at me, then at a barely discernable path at the edge of the camp.

"Walk," he said.

Our procession continued for a distance of perhaps two hundred yards. I could no longer see or hear any sign of the camp.

At Alejandro's direction, his associate fixed one end of the chain around the thick trunk of a palm tree and attached the other end to my left leg.

The guerrilla leader again stared into my eyes. "This will give you something to think about. We will return in two hours."

He turned abruptly and walked away, followed by the others. About ten yards away, the two armed guerrillas stopped and took up positions to watch me.

The two hours passed. Then the evening. And then the night, and the next day, and the day after that. Except for a change of shift of the guards every ten hours and the daily delivery of one serving of yucca roots, I saw no one. No one spoke to me. I was alone.

I was in for a long wait.

The days turned into weeks. I was wet and cold. My clothes began to rot. The meager rations of roots took a toll on my health. I developed diverticulitis, a digestive disorder that causes abdominal pain, cramps, fevers, nausea, chills, and—when allowed to fester—internal hemorrhaging. My body was deteriorating.

There was little I could do about my physical condition, but I took what measures I could to exercise my intellect. My work in grafting an improved cocoa plant stock, along with hybrids of avocados and other citrus fruits, had done more than provide the backbone of our cooperative efforts—it had also enabled me to refine my technique for one of my favorite hobbies, producing orchid hybrids. Now I scanned the jungle canopy in order to identify and classify orchids. I located about thirty varieties, either *cattleya, dendrobium,* or *odontoglossum.*

I watched as the orchid stems slowly reached into the light of the jungle canopy and unfolded their buds. I imagined how I would cross-fertilize each and what type of flower would result. Then I turned to the leaves, trees, and vines, classifying each of these as well. These were games to keep my mind alert.

I also turned to music. I enjoy the classical works of Chopin, Tchaikovsky, Haydn, and Bach—particularly Bach's Goldberg Variations performed by pianist Glenn Gould. I recalled these and could hear every note in my head—at least until evening thunderstorms interrupted my reveries.

To enrich my spirit, I thought back to translations of the New Testament in Barí with Bobby, Kaymiyokba, and so many others. I remembered the marvelous experiences of trying to communicate the concepts of Christianity in the vernacular of the Motilone people. And I recalled how sweetly they responded to God's compassion and call to be like His Son. These were encouraging memories.

As the weeks wore on, I felt totally broken. I received no correspondence, no contact from the outside world. I began to feel as though everyone had forgotten me, even though my intellect told me the Motilones would never forget me. But even though I felt abandoned, I was not angry with God. I was disappointed in myself. Perhaps if I had been more intelligent or coy, the guerrillas would not have captured me. Maybe I should have been more intent to reconcile conflicts with the colonists, which would have prevented them from throwing in with the guerrillas. Maybe I had not done all that I could have done.

Either way, I had the peace of God's sovereignty. I had to remember that.

As I entered what I estimated to be the fourth month of my confinement to the palm tree, I moved closer to the edge of reality. I was terribly lonely. I wanted to play a role, not be the victim of someone's anger and hate. I had always been able to find a way to be a part of something. With a friend. Within a community. Someone would offer me ideas or compassion or a place within their group, and I would share something of myself in return. This interaction with people—belonging and sharing—is *life*.

Now that had been taken from me. I desperately yearned to belong again.

The jungle animals were the only living creatures left to me. I had learned to mimic the sounds made by parrots. I called to them, and some ventured to the lower limbs of nearby trees. Eventually, a few of these even flew to the ground, only two yards away. I talked to them in Barí, telling them of my anguish. "If I had wings like you," I said, "I'd fly away. But my feet are heavy." The parrots seemed to answer me. "Pull your foot out of the hoop," one said. I tried but could not.

"Give me your freedom to fly over the jungle," I said. A parrot replied, "I will take your spirit with me." He flew away. I felt that a part of me went with him.

Another day, a band of capuchin monkeys surrounded me. I chatted with them, and they also came out of the trees for a closer look. I put out my right hand—not open, because that is considered a threat, but with the back facing them. One monkey stretched out a delicate finger and touched my knuckles. Even this brief contact with another of God's creatures was invigorating.

"You have your freedom. I don't," I said to him. "Take my spirit with you."

The monkey replied, "I will travel with you." I sensed him sweeping me up into the trees. I inhaled the scent of the wet jungle and felt the rush of wind blowing through my hair. Peering through the leaves, I saw my body far below, that poor fellow still chained to the palm tree. I wished I could help him.

And then, suddenly, I was no longer flying overhead. I was back on the jungle floor, tired, ill, hungry, and once more alone.

Perhaps my "flights" over the jungle were hallucinations, though they seemed real enough at the time. I have never known for certain. Later, the guerrillas who guarded me said they had never seen anyone attract parrots and monkeys out of the trees and converse with the animals as I did.

Despite these diversions, my situation was growing more desperate. The diverticulitis had intensified. In addition to the headaches, chills, and stomach cramps, I was bleeding internally. It appeared that I was going to die here, shackled to a palm tree in the jungle. Thoughts of the Motilones, the people I loved and who loved me, kept me struggling to live. I longed to be with them.

The jungle animals were the only living
creatures left to me. I had learned to mimic
the sounds made by parrots. I called to
them, and some ventured to the lower
limbs of nearby trees.

As I contemplated these things one evening, cold, hungry, and discouraged, I raised my head and spied a movement. There, about eight yards above me in the trees, was a Motilone Indian wearing a loincloth. I didn't recognize him, but I was thrilled to see him.

There was something strange about his position. I squinted my eyes, trying to get a better view. I realized that he wasn't grasping the limbs of the trees. I didn't understand how it was possible, but he appeared to be suspended in space.

The Motilone hummed and whistled to me in Barí. Because the Motilones employ a tonal language, communicating through a combination of high, mid, and low tones, I understood what he was saying. No words were articulated for the guards to hear.

"The tribal elders have asked me to find you," he said.

"Be careful," I whistled back. "The guards will see you. They have fire sticks." But the guards didn't seem to notice. The Motilone was well camouflaged behind branches and leaves.

"If you release me from the tree, then encircle the camp and shoot some arrows, I may be able to escape," I whistled.

"No," he responded. "That is not why I am here. I have come to stop the disease inside you. I come to give you warmth."

Immediately, I felt a change within my body. The cramps subsided. I *was* warmer. And I sensed that somehow the internal bleeding had ceased as well.

"You will be released," the Motilone whistled, "but not yet. It will be soon, at the proper time."

I was overwhelmed. Something inexplicable, supernatural, was happening. I put my head down, which is the Motilone way of honoring the person before you. When I brought my head back up, he was gone.

Growing up, I had never understood angels. To me, they were something carved in a stone altar or depicted in Renaissance art, nothing more. I had read about them in the Bible, but I could never quite bring myself to believe in them.

It appeared that I was going to die here,
shackled to a palm tree in the jungle.
Thoughts of the Motilones, the people
I loved and who loved me, kept me
struggling to live.

When I was translating the New Testament into Barí, I attempted to explain the concept of angels to the Motilones. "But I really do not understand angels," I said. "I don't know how to translate this into your language."

They grinned. "We know what you are trying to say to us," one said. "You're speaking of a *ChigBarí*—a messenger sent by God. It can have a physical body or be a spirit." The Motilones understood angels better than I did.

The Motilone in the trees, I was sure, was a *ChigBarí*. And I was overjoyed that God had answered the prayers of my friends through this messenger of healing and hope. No matter how desperate and alone I felt, God was with me. He still loved me. I could still entrust my life to Him.

The next day, after four months of misery and isolation, the guerrillas unshackled me from the tree and brought me back into their camp. The worst was over.

Or so I thought.

Chapter 12

"You Are One of Us"

I walk on the trail of life experiences to the horizons. No evil spirit can threaten me or take me from the security I know in Jesus. I am suspended in Jesus through my expression of faith.

—Song of the Motilones

I sat on the ground, my hands tied in front of me. I'd been clothed in camouflage, the same as the guerrillas. Members of the opposition forces walked past without even glancing my way. Several carried weapons.

It was the spring of 1989, a few days after my release from the palm tree. I had observed about seventy rebels in the camp. Most were in training for combat. A few were recovering from previous confrontations with government troops. They were treated by ELN physicians and nurses under palm-thatched canopies hidden beneath the trees. I did not know what the guerrillas had planned for me now. I wasn't sure that they knew either.

With nothing else to do, I picked up a stick and traced, as well as I could with my hands bound, the letter *A* in the dirt. *A* is the most significant letter in the Barí language. It stands for speech and life. Every Motilone name ends with this vowel. It means he or she possesses life.

A pair of worn boots appeared in front of me. I looked up. It was a guerrilla, probably in his early twenties, with loose straight hair, a narrow mouth, and an expression that evoked respect. He had a pistol tucked into his belt. He was examining my scratches in the dirt with a penetrating eye.

The guerrilla crouched down, picked up another stick, and, copying my work, traced his own *A*.

"Ah," I said.

"Ah," he repeated.

Now I wrote "mamá" in the dirt—Spanish for mother. Again, the guerrilla traced the letters. So I wrote "amo mí" in front of mamá—I love my mother. He copied this, too, and I read it aloud. His face softened and acquired a faraway look. Then he focused back on me, his eyes shining with satisfaction.

I basked in the warmth of his expression. Here was a revolutionary who looted banks, shot helicopters out of the sky, and sabotaged oil pipelines—a man trained to kill—yet he was tender about his mother. He obviously could not read or write, yet he had an interest in literacy, in learning. This was more than a cold, calculating enemy. I was dealing with a human being again.

Later, I was able to write down other short phrases on paper that my new "friend" also copied. One of the camp *responsables*, as the guerrillas called their officers, observed this interaction and asked if I would consider teaching literacy to more of the guerrillas. So we started a simple school, an hour and a half each day. It was the beginning of a change in my relationship with my captors.

I became a camp cook, learning quickly that all of the cooking had to be done during the night when the smoke was undetectable. Everything was cooked by 3:00 a.m. and then eaten the following day.

Over time, I taught the other cooks how to make sauces out of smoked palm grubs. I showed them how to dry banana skins in the sun and grind them into flour. I used this flour to make green banana bread for the camp three times a week. I showed others how to produce an elixir effective in controlling diarrhea by grinding selected leaves. I helped them produce a natural oil from tree bark that relieves asthma. Because I knew how to extract teeth with forceps, I became the camp dentist. I even wrote flowery love letters for the illiterate rebels to send to their sweethearts.

Meanwhile, the literacy classes were invigorating for the guerrillas and for me. They led to a whole curriculum of study: reading and writing, ecology, history, geography, and social and political sciences. Many of the guerrillas had received little or no schooling and were eager to prove themselves. We discussed socialism and communism, dialectical materialism and democracy. I explained the history of liberation theology—the school of thought that focuses on Jesus as a liberator and deliverer of justice—that had provided the impetus for the rise of the left-wing rebel movements.

The responsables encouraged my teaching. They interpreted my interest as evidence that I was coming around to their way of thinking. Many of the officers attended classes as well. I was careful not to overtly inject my values into our discussions. I knew that my time as instructor would end abruptly if I was too candid or forceful.

Once when I was teaching on socialism, one of the responsables pulled out an elastic band from an old sock, and he crouched down while I was talking. Everyone else in the room was rather serious but he was relaxed. *He's not even paying attention to what I'm saying*, I thought.

The responsable pulled back on the rubber band and began snapping it at the ants that scurried about on the floor. He shot several of them about twenty inches across the floor. With each snap, the students murmured their amusement. *Well, I'm happy that everyone is relaxed,* I thought to myself, *but I wish they were paying attention.* So I asked them a question. To my surprise, the responsable stood up, looked me in the eye, and gave me a precise, direct answer that summed up my entire talk. He had heard *everything.*

It reminded me to watch my step, but it also encouraged me. Oftentimes when we are working in an area where we think people are distracted, we don't realize that in their hearts there is a hunger for God's Word. We can't judge books by their covers. They are watching and listening even when we don't think so.

Eventually, the guerrillas asked about my motivations and why I didn't hate them for "depriving me of my liberty." It was a clear opportunity to talk about my faith, but I resisted their questions at first. Something told me the time wasn't right, and I had learned to obey these inner impulses, knowing that God gave them to me for a reason.

A couple of weeks later, I was allowed to have a Bible. It became very precious to me. Through my translation work, I had already committed much of the New Testament to memory—but to have God's Word in my hands again was an unbelievable blessing. Again and again I turned to the Psalms for strength and reassurance:

> "Because he loves me," says the LORD, "I will rescue him; I will protect him, for he acknowledges my name. He will call upon me, and I will answer him; I will be with him in trouble, I will deliver him and honor him."
>
> —PSALM 91:14–15

Not long after—and only on Sundays, so as not to appear overly intrusive or evangelistic—I began to answer the guerrillas' questions about God and my personal faith. As I talked about what Christ meant to me, I noticed tears in the eyes of several guerrillas. Despite their violent training, these were idealistic, even thoughtful, men. The love and compassion of Jesus meant something to them.

A few of these men accepted Christ. These were profound moments in my experience as a captive, times when God's Spirit manifested Himself so beautifully, so tenderly, that hardened terrorists often broke down and wept as they received Him into their lives. For me, the most touching part was that it was not my concept of God they accepted; it was the very real, very personal Jesus Christ who met them within the context of their own experiences, culture, and understanding.

This was a clear opportunity to talk about my faith, but I resisted their questions at first. Something told me the time wasn't right.

I felt privileged to witness these conversions. Incredibly, some of my captors had become my brothers.

I never told these new Christians that they had to leave the guerrilla movement, though they sometimes asked me if they should. Instead I told them: "You belong to Jesus Christ now. You must answer to Him, and to society."

Soon I had evidence that Christ was indeed speaking to these young men. A Christian guerrilla crept to my hammock late at night and shook me awake. "Papa Bruchko," he whispered, "I have heard that you may be executed." I was silent at this disturbing message. It was not good news, but it was hard to know what to believe anymore.

The young believer kept whispering. "I want to tell you that if I am ordered to execute you, I have decided to refuse." This meant, of course, that he himself would be executed for disobeying an order. "I am with you," he said, "even if it costs me my life."

I knew this man, and I believed him. His words moved me deeply. I felt the strong presence of Jesus that night and was comforted.

After that, I shuttled from camp to camp, continuing my classes with some of the same students while meeting many new ones. I gained a measure of trust and was allowed at times to walk freely within the camps. On one of these occasions, I ventured near a stream where several guerrillas were bathing. Suddenly I saw, only a few feet to my right, a submachine gun mounted on a tripod. The idea immediately leapt to my mind—I could grab the gun, shoot the guerrillas in the stream, and make an escape.

But I made no move. Hadn't I denounced killing in our discussions? And if I escaped, the guerrillas would only capture me again, unless I left the country. But what would that accomplish? My home was in the jungle. My family was the Motilones. Escape was not a solution to the problem. I had achieved an almost tolerable existence with the guerrillas. It was better to remain where I was and see what God had in mind.

Unfortunately, my improved relations with the guerrillas soon took a turn for the worse.

One morning I heard sharp hand claps—the equivalent for knocking on doors in the Latin American jungles. A responsable and a man with a hood over his face approached. There was something familiar about the walk and build of the hooded man.

"This man wishes to speak to you," the responsable said to me.

At that moment, I put it together. "Hello, Manuel Pérez," I said to the "anonymous" visitor.

"You think this is Manuel Pérez?" the responsable said.

"I know it is."

Pérez, amused by the attempted prank, yanked off his hood. "Hello, Bruce Olson," he said.

Pérez, a former Jesuit priest from Spain, was the leader of the ELN movement. Years before, we had taken university classes in liberation theology together in Bogotá. I had enjoyed his company then, and we had gotten to know each other well. We had nearly identical assessments of the social and political challenges facing Colombia. Since then, however, he had embraced the violent methods of the guerrilla movement as the solution to these problems.

Pérez told me he was surprised when he learned of my abduction. It had been ordered by a regional responsable, not by the governing ELN leadership. But he offered no apologies for my situation.

We talked for a while, then walked into the jungle and sat on a fallen log. The setting was deceptively tranquil.

"Bruce, you have had excellent success with your cooperatives, first with the Indians, and now with the Spanish-speaking nationals," he said. "The profits you have earned and dedicated to people in the region have provided remarkable benefits. I commend you."

I nodded but said nothing.

"It is the determination of our board of responsables that we also need cooperatives to finance our operations and to provide social development for the regions we control, which eventually will include the entire country. If you join with us, this will be your responsibility. You will establish our cooperative programs and direct the distribution of profits for the people. You will be allowed to continue your work with the Indians, but you will also have these other obligations. It will be a great opportunity to serve all the people of Colombia."

I contemplated my bound hands before answering.

"I appreciate what you are saying, Manuel," I said. "And I support what you are trying to do. But I believe offering social development without the conscience of Christ is just changing the environment, the surroundings. Presenting an economic solution to social problems does not alter a person on the inside. If an individual's heart does not change, nothing is really accomplished."

"I am a priest. I understand that. But we have rejected the positions of the church and its theology. Only through armed revolution can we bring about the changes in society that must be made. We will change the environment, and then people will decide if they wish to change on the inside."

I shook my head. "I'm sorry. My morality, my conscience, does not allow me to work with those who would kill their enemies."

"That is your decision?"

"Yes."

Pérez lowered his voice. His tone was gentle, though the words were not. "You do understand what happens to those who will not align themselves with our programs?"

I knew exactly what he meant.

"Yes," I said.

Pérez examined a palm tree a few feet away. I thought I detected sadness in his expression. Then he clapped me on the shoulder and stood. "Well, you'll be here for a while yet. Think about it."

A few weeks later, long after Pérez had left the camp, the local responsables insisted that I make a decision: join the movement or face execution.

I refused to join. I could not justify killing to attain social and political goals. I knew that my refusal meant a death sentence. I was not eager to die, but I would not turn my back on the teachings and compassion of Christ.

"Presenting an economic solution to social problems does not alter a person on the inside. If an individual's heart does not change, nothing is really accomplished."

The guerrillas next pressured me to sign a public "confession" of my crimes against humanity. The charges they conjured up were ludicrous: I had murdered more than six thousand Motilones; I was trafficking in cocaine; I had enslaved the indigenous people to work in my gold and emerald mines; I was a CIA spy; I'd flown in helicopter attacks against the rebels. According to their charges, I had even taught American astronauts how to speak in Barí so the Russians wouldn't understand what they were saying in space.

Knowing that the autonomy and independence of the Motilones would be taken from them if I were to sign their ludicrous confession, I determined that I would rather die. "I refuse to sign the 'confession,'" I said. "I've done nothing,"

"Then we will kill you," I was told.

I lowered my head, but lifted my eyes in an expression of defiance that was louder than words.

The rebels tried to break me, using an assortment of ploys. They began with psychology. "The Indians have totally abandoned you," they told me repeatedly. "Your programs are in disarray. We've talked to them, and not a single one cares whether you live or die. You might as well save yourself, because no one else will."

I couldn't believe that the Motilones would abandon me after almost thirty years together. Surely they would remember all that we had been through. Surely they would continue the work we had begun in the jungle. It was, after all, not *my* work but theirs and God's. As the guerrillas repeated their assertions, however, I began to doubt. Was it possible?

Then came the "good cop/bad cop" approach. Some guerrillas were especially kind and friendly to me. Others were crude and cruel. Both tried unsuccessfully to coerce me into championing their cause or influencing the Indians toward them.

While this was going on within the guerrilla camp, the armed forces set off sixteen bombs on two different occasions to try and hinder the rebel forces. To be in the midst of a rebel camp under military attack was very traumatic, to say the least. First the military forces sent in slow-flying DC-3 airplanes with equipment that could locate body heat. As soon as they detected the presence of guerrillas, the jet bombers would fly in and strike.

When the guerrillas saw the DC-3 airplanes, they scattered in every direction. There was no time to ask questions; they would just jump up and run. Every time I saw this happen, I ran behind them as fast as I could. Then the jets with the bombs would fly in. *BOOM!* The whole earth would shake, the trees would swoon, and the parrots would cry in agony.

The armed forces sent in these bombs for their own advantage. They were not against me, but they certainly were not going to sacrifice anything for me, either. It was harrowing to endure, but I was about to face an even greater challenge.

I was turned over to the guerrillas I called "thugs." I was to be punished for my lack of cooperation. Their instruments were huge dowels made from the trunks of trees. These must have weighed close to one hundred pounds each. I was made to lie down, and the dowels were rolled repeatedly over my body, three or four times a day. I could feel my insides being crushed. They fractured my ribs and caused me to urinate and vomit blood. Even now I can barely write about these terrible memories.

Afterward, I could hardly walk or breathe. Once, I was forced to march three hours to another camp where a man who gave massages was sent to me. When he saw the bruises all over my body, a look of shame came over his face. "This is not revolution," he whispered to me. "We shouldn't be hurting and torturing people. But I am not a commanding officer."

Later, I suffered excruciating pain and eventually lost consciousness. When I awoke, a masked physician was examining me. He discovered that I was bleeding internally again. He said that I had lost so much blood that I needed a transfusion immediately or I would die.

I did not want the transfusion. I was ready to die. But I wasn't given a choice.

As I lay in a hammock, I heard an argument break out among the guerrillas. They were fighting over who would have the honor of giving their blood to "Papa Bruchko," as they had taken to calling me, probably because I was the oldest man in the camp. Finally a young guerrilla, Camillo, won the argument. His blood was A positive, like mine.

It took a long time for that transfusion. First they put a needle in Camillo's arm. I remember that this soldier of the revolution, who had fought many battles, cringed when the needle was inserted. I thought to myself, *Good. I hope it hurts a lot.* His blood went through a filter, and then was transferred into a tube that ran into my arm.

At one point our eyes met. In the past, I had seen Camillo hanging around as I led classes for the guerrillas, but we had not spoken. Now, I tried to read his expression. There was an intensity there I did not understand.

I must have fallen asleep, because I awoke in the middle of the night, alone and in pain. I tried to separate myself from it, but this time I couldn't. I felt empty and hollow. The intensity of my physical pain only increased the sadness I felt for everything I had experienced in the past few months.

Then the strangest thing happened: an Andean mockingbird known as a *mirla* began to sing. The mirla never sings at night, yet this one's melody went on and on. It was hauntingly beautiful and familiar somehow. The music was complex, set in a minor key. I strained to identify it.

Suddenly I understood—it was a tonal Motilone chant! The mirla had heard the Motilones singing and mimicked their tones. I listened closer. The meaning of the song was, "I walk on the trail of life experiences to the horizons. No evil spirit can threaten me or take me from the security I know in Jesus. I am suspended in Jesus through my expression of faith."

I wondered if I was hallucinating or if this was another angel sent by God. It didn't matter. The music restored my spirit. Just a few hours before, I had wanted to die. Now I felt myself coming back to life. I spied the full moon, its light pouring down through the thick jungle vegetation. It seemed as if it were shining just for me.

In the morning, the sun's first rays filtered through the jungle canopy into the camp, casting everything in a greenish hue. I was wrapped in my hammock like an enchilada when I heard soft footsteps.

Suddenly the hammock parted, and a face filled my vision. It was Camillo. His nose almost touched mine; I could smell his foul breath.

"Bruce Olson, do you know who I am?" he inquired in a loud voice.

"Yes," I said. "You are the valiant Camillo."

"Oh, but I am more than that," he said. "Twenty-four years ago, my father, Don Jorge, committed suicide. My mother was left a widow with several children, including me. You and the Motilones sent food from the cooperatives—rice, beans, tomato juice, macaroni, sugar, and even delicacies such as peach nectar and crackers—to my family for two years without ever asking for payment.

"Many years ago, you saved my life. Now I am repaying you. I gave you my blood and kept you alive. You have guerrilla blood in your veins. You are one of us."

The music restored my spirit. Just a few
hours before, I had wanted to die. Now I
felt myself coming back to life.

Then Camillo embraced me. It was the first expression of warm, physical human contact I'd had since I was abducted. I melted like wax in a fire. Who could have imagined all those years ago that a simple expression of compassion from the heart would one day save my life? Only God could have reconciled these two situations so beautifully. I felt His presence more closely than ever. I had endured hunger, suffering, and pain at the hands of my captors. But I did not hate them. And it was not my role to judge them.

Camillo was right. Despite my refusals to align myself with their movement, I had indeed, in a way, become one of them. I now had guerrilla blood flowing through me and had experienced the warmth of their embrace. Though we usually failed to recognize it, we were all somehow linked in a common struggle to find solutions to our mutual problems: me, Camillo, the Motilones and other indigenous tribes, Manuel Pérez and the guerrillas, the entire citizenry of Colombia. It was a difficult concept to accept—and at the same time, a great comfort.

Chapter 13

Immature Brothers

Only someone who is immature chooses to kill those who oppose him.
—Kaymiyokba

It was July 1989. I had been escorted to a meeting with the responsable wearing the red beret—Alejandro. It was a short visit.

"Bruce Olson, our patience with you has ended," he said. "You have refused to assist us in establishing a dialogue with the Motilones, you have refused to accept your responsibility as a member of our movement, and you have refused to admit to your crimes against the people. You will be executed. You have three days to prepare yourself."

I stiffened. After months in captivity, the end had suddenly arrived.

"There is nothing special that I need to do," I said. "I'm ready. Why don't you just get it over with?"

Alejandro waved his hand at me as if swatting away a bug. "Three days," he said, and ordered me taken away.

I spent what were to be my last hours on earth doing exactly what I had done in the previous weeks—teaching, cooking, going about daily life as usual. If it was God's will for me to die, I could accept death. After my ordeal as a hostage, execution sounded more like a relief than a sentence.

The guerrillas watched me closely during those three days. I wondered what they were thinking. By this time more than half the camp had given their lives to Jesus. The responsables, I thought, would have a hard time finding someone to shoot me. Even many of those who weren't Christians had become my friends. I worried about them, as I worried about the Motilones. But I knew that God would complete the work He had begun in all their lives. My mission was over.

I knew what lay ahead of me at the end of three days' time. During my captivity I had witnessed five executions. One was a German rancher abducted for ransom. Abandoned by his wife and family, he wanted to confess his sins to me before he died, but I directed him to make his heart right with God by confessing directly to Him. The vivid memory of his execution still haunts me.

Another had been a policeman, but he had blackmailed people and had even kidnapped a little girl for ransom. The people of the town complained of his cruelty, so the guerrillas abducted him to make the town people happy and win their allegiance. Before his execution, he asked me to tell his wife and children that he loved them. After his death, his body was disfigured and put on display in front of the police station where he had been stationed.

Another man was tortured for days until he died. He requested that I remain with him throughout the ordeal because my presence brought him comfort. As difficult as it was to witness such an atrocity, I stayed with him in his agony, offering whatever comfort God could minister through me.

The worst moments of my captivity were those spent watching the executions of the other hostages—people who had become my friends. As they were torn apart by firing squad bullets, I was told, "This is what will happen to you if you do not sign a confession." There are no words to describe the painfulness of these experiences.

Now it was my turn.

The morning of my execution was like any July day in the jungle. It had rained the night before. Pockets of steam rose into the air from places where the sun had broken through the canopy and struck the damp ground. I took a deep breath, relishing for one last time the fragrance of the jungle leaves that had always reminded me of the earthy savor of underground truffles.

It seemed like any other day, except that no one spoke to me. Perhaps they did not know what to say.

I found it difficult not to dwell on my shortcomings, so I turned to my Bible. I spent a few minutes reading the Psalms. One of them was Psalm 100: "Enter his gates with thanksgiving and his courts with praise; give thanks to him and praise his name. For the LORD is good and his love endures forever; his faithfulness continues through all generations" (vv. 4–5).

> I knew what lay ahead of me at the end
> of three days' time. During my captivity
> I had witnessed five executions.

I thanked God for enhancing my life by placing me in South America and joining me with the Motilones. I thanked Him for providing relationships and warmth of family—including the guerrillas who had become like brothers to me. I thanked Him that even here, among those who tortured and killed to achieve their purposes, I had shared life and felt His strong presence.

At mid-morning, there was a stirring in the camp. Alejandro and two of his associates walked briskly in my direction. I was ordered to accompany them to a small clearing, where I was tied to a tree.

One of the responsables began reading the charges against me, the same ridiculous statements I had heard before, while Alejandro and the others left to round up the firing squad. The responsable in front of me declared that I had been sentenced to death by the "people's court." Then he stepped forward with a blindfold.

"No," I said, shaking my head. "No blindfold." I wanted to look my executioners in the eyes.

Over the guerrilla's shoulder, I saw that Alejandro had returned with a group of guerrillas carrying rifles. But there was a disturbance. One of them seemed to be arguing with the responsable.

It was Camillo. I could hear some of the exchange. "Olson refuses to accept our social values," Alejandro said. "He will not accept responsibility to align the Indians with us."

"But it was my blood that kept him alive!" Camillo said.

"Yes," Alejandro said. "But we can no longer maintain him. And if he is released, he will become our enemy and bring in armed forces."

Camillo lost the argument. He and nine others with rifles—most of them new Christians—were ordered to stand in a line about ten yards in front of me. Slowly they shuffled into formation, Camillo somewhere in the middle. Many had their heads down.

These men were my brothers in Christ, and now they would shoot me. It was shocking to me to realize that they were about to raise their arms to execute me, but I tried to understand their dilemma. In the code of the guerrillas, there was no room for ambiguity. If they refused their orders, they too would be executed.

Still, I couldn't help thinking that if I were a guerrilla who had become a Christian, I would refuse the orders and let them execute me as well. It was heartbreaking to me that they would not do the same. But I have never walked in their shoes.

Perhaps this way is better, I reasoned. *If I am to be executed, it is best that it be done by a brother in the faith.*

One of the responsables went down the line and handed out cartridges. There was a loud "click" as each slid into a rifle chamber.

Finally, the order came to raise weapons. I braced myself, stood as straight as I could, and faced the ten men before me. Several had tears in their eyes. One of these was Camillo. I focused on him last.

A responsable started the count: "Five. Four—"

O God, You are forever faithful!

"Three. Two—"

Take me into Your arms!

"One. Fire!"

My ears filled with the deafening sound of rifle reports. And I felt…nothing.

The men in the firing squad stared at me. I stared back.

One of the men brought his rifle up to his face and examined it, a bewildered expression on his face. Suddenly he exclaimed, "They were blanks!"

In unison, the firing squad and I swiveled our heads toward Alejandro. He was watching me intently. Our eyes met. Almost imperceptibly, he nodded. Then, without a word to me or his men, he turned and walked away.

It had been a cruel ruse, one last attempt to break me. They had hoped I would change my mind, beg for my life, and choose to cooperate.

The ruse had failed. But after preparing myself emotionally and spiritually for death, I felt exhausted and disappointed. I had thought I was going to heaven. Instead, I was still here, still a prisoner. Nothing had changed.

Camillo stepped forward to untie me. With the others watching, he did not speak. But his eyes danced.

He helped me back to my hammock. "I was ready to die," I said quietly after lying down.

"I know," he whispered. "But God has His ways. I see that now more than ever. He must have another plan—for both of us."

He pulled me closer. "I never pulled the trigger," he whispered in my ear. Then he embraced me and walked away.

> # Camillo lost the argument. He and nine others with rifles—most of them new Christians—were ordered to stand in a line about ten yards in front of me.

A few days later another responsable, Federico, came to me. "Bruce Olson, I have good news for you! You are being released. Are you happy?"

I was suspicious. I shrugged my shoulders and said, "I'm indifferent. My concern is for the Motilone people, the solidarity of their traditional life and the protection of their territory, which is so vital to their future. What about them?"

"Yes, yes, we understand your commitment," Federico said. "We made an error when we kidnapped you. The charges against you have been dropped. It's an embarrassment to us that you've been held in our camps. If we've mistreated you, we hope you can find the grace to forgive us. We've decided to leave the Motilones as an autonomous people. You may continue your work among them as before."

I was incredulous. "Are there conditions to my release?"

"You are released without conditions," Federico said. "*Now* are you happy?"

"If this is true, I am indeed."

Federico's eyes actually filled with tears. Then he hugged me.

Two weeks later, after a long trek back to civilization through the jungle and rivers, I was finally released to a group of journalists on the Colombia-Venezuela border. It was July 19, 1989, nine months after I had been abducted.

I was free.

I immediately made my way to Iquiacarora to rejoin the Motilones. As I came from the higher mountains to the foothills where the trails are much more defined and you can see a further distance away, Cuadudura spotted me. She related in the tonal language of the Motilones, "Yado, Bruchko, is alive and he is walking to our house."

The musical sound of her voice echoed in the jungle and valleys. As I heard it, there was only one thought going through my mind: *I survived.*

All the people and the children ran to the trail to greet me, but it wasn't an immediate euphoria of hugs as one might imagine. They simply drew near to me in a respectful manner, waiting for me to make the first gesture. I hesitated for a moment while I gained control of my emotions. Then I went over and touched them on the shoulders and stomachs—a Motilone sign of affection. They broke out into shouts of jubilation. It was a joyous reunion.

I quickly learned that the Motilones had not abandoned me at all, as I had briefly feared. Instead, they had joined forces with the other indigenous tribes in the region and threatened war with the guerrillas unless I was released. A delegation of Indians traveled to Bogotá to meet with editors of *El Tiempo*, the country's leading newspaper. They arranged for a full-page statement in a Sunday edition entitled "A Norwegian Motilone cries out for freedom." It denounced the charges made against me by the ELN and called for my release so the programs we'd begun could continue. They sent a copy of this statement to my friends and supporters in the United States and around the world, establishing an international network of prayer support.[1]

In addition, the Indians published an open letter to the ELN in the nation's major newspapers. It read, in part:

> Today we are asking for the life and quick return of a friend, a white man, a "foreigner," [and] as you badly call him a "conqueror." Thirty-five years is a lifetime sharing the heat, the rain, the sickness, the sorrows, and the glories of each of our little triumphs.... We give thanks to our good friend Bruce who in good or bad times always was with us, so we call him brother.... Bruce is our friend and counselor who always has been on our side coordinating and helping the development of the world of all the Motilones. We ask today on behalf of all the people of the United Catatumbo the prompt homecoming of Bruce Olson, a valuable person, so with the help of God he can continue the changes that have come to Colombia.[2]

At this point the media took up the cause, running hundreds of front-page stories in every newspaper in the nation. Headlines such as "Free Olson, the 'Motilone'" were commonplace. Television and radio stations repeatedly aired short segments calling for my release. A well-known Colombian priest, as well as the International Red Cross and the Colombian Peace, Justice, and Life Committee, also joined in efforts to secure my freedom.

Then the Colombian populace responded, rising up as a single voice to denounce the guerrillas for what they were doing. "How can these criminals claim to speak for 'the people' and then kidnap a man who has done more for the indigenous people of this nation than anyone else?" they asked in letters to the papers. "It's an outrage!"[3]

As I celebrated with the Motilones, I was overwhelmed to learn of these developments. It seemed as if the whole world had heard of my captivity and fought for my release.

Eventually, half wondering if the tribal elders would think I was crazy, I brought up the visit of the Motilone angel when I was shackled to the tree.

"Yes, we know all about that," one of the elders said.

"You do?" I asked.

I quickly learned that the Motilones had
not abandoned me at all, as I had briefly
feared. Instead, they had joined forces with
the other indigenous tribes in the region
and threatened war with the guerrillas
unless I was released.

"Of course," he said. "We sent ChigBarí to you, and he returned to tell us
where you were. We were relieved to learn that you were alive."

I did not understand this, but I didn't question it either. It was a spiritual matter, and in some spiritual areas—particularly involving angels—the Motilones
knew things that I did not. I simply considered it a blessing that they cared this
much for me.

A couple of days later, a helicopter flew overhead and landed near Iquiacarora.
President Barco, I was told by a government official, wished to interview me.
Soon I was on my way to Bogotá, accompanied by several Motilones who decided
to join me.

Our entire delegation met in the president's office. He recounted the history
of my nearly three decades with the Motilones, offering generous platitudes
about the progress we had made in establishing a pilot program for all indigenous people to follow. Then he reviewed the history of the rebel movements
and the terror and havoc they were creating for Colombia's people, armed forces,
economy, government, and society.

"The guerrillas are terrorists. They want only to destroy everything that you
have achieved," President Barco said to the Motilones and me. "If not for the
support and public outcry led by the Motilones, our enemies would have killed
you, Bruce. That's why we must eliminate—"

"Our immature brothers," a voice interjected, "spared Bruchko because of
their fear over how we would have responded."

Both President Barco and I turned toward the speaker. It was Kaymiyokba.

There was silence for a moment. Then the president, glancing first at
Kaymiyokba and then at me, said, "Perhaps this is so. But 'immature brothers'?
Why call them that?"

"The Motilones view the guerrillas as Colombian brothers, not as enemies," I said. "They only want the violence to end and would prefer to see them reintegrated back into society."

Kaymiyokba nodded. "Only someone who is immature chooses to kill those who oppose him."

Once again, President Barco was silent. He was surprised to be spoken to in this manner, and at this conciliatory attitude toward a group who had held me, an esteemed friend of the Motilones, for so many months.

I, on the other hand, was pleased. Kaymiyokba's words put the situation into perspective. The guerrillas were more than enemies, more than a nuisance to be exterminated like termites that have infested a home. They were human beings, people with intellect and emotion and dreams. Certainly neither I nor the Motilones condoned their methods, but the reasons for their concerns were legitimate. In a way, the guerrillas were like children throwing a temper tantrum, angry and trying to attract attention in the only way they knew. Immature, yes. But created by God and still deserving of the opportunity to join His eternal family.

The Motilones had given the president of Colombia something to think about.

In the ensuing days, I was the subject of a press conference and was interviewed by television, radio, and print media. I was astonished at the attention I received. I left my hotel for some fresh air and walked to an automated teller machine to withdraw cash. A couple walked by, staring. One of them said to the other, "That's Bruce Olson, the man who was kidnapped by the guerrillas." Before I knew it, a crowd had gathered. Everyone was friendly, offering words of support or asking questions, but I began to feel cornered. I escaped to the street and hailed a taxi.

"You're Bruce Olson!" the driver said after I got in. "We have all been praying for you." Back in the hotel lobby, another guest recognized me. "Please remain in Colombia," she said. "You are an inspiration to us."

During my captivity, many people heard about my work with the Motilones for the first time and appreciated that a white man would try to improve the lives of Colombia's indigenous peoples. And they learned that I had become a Colombian citizen in 1971, which endeared me to them even more. According to one of the newspaper editors I met later, I was a household name, a hero. Even the newspaper crossword puzzles and comic strips featured "Bruce Olson."

My popularity was not universal, however. Some of the most violent rebel factions again threatened to kill me if I returned to the jungle. Though I wanted to go back, I did not wish to foolishly risk my life or endanger the Motilones. At this same time, my mother and family requested that I come back to the United States. And so I did.

> The guerrillas were more than enemies,
> more than a nuisance to be exterminated
> like termites that have infested a home.
> They were human beings, people with
> intellect and emotion and dreams.

Yet I left Colombia with great sadness. Would I ever return to the Motilones, to the place I felt was home?

I needed spiritual guidance. I am not usually in the habit of asking for signs from God, but this time I made an exception. My strong desire was to be back in Colombia among the Motilones, yet I knew I had to be obedient to His will. There would have to be a place and purpose for me there. I asked for some confirmation one way or the other—that I should stay in the United States or return to my adopted country and family.

A week later, I received a phone call from President Barco. "Bruce," he said, "if the guerrillas are immature brothers, then there must be something to reconcile. We are forming a national peace commission that will attempt to work out nonviolent solutions to our problems. Four of the guerrilla organizations have agreed to participate, and one—a faction of the ELN, the group that abducted you—has requested your presence as well. You have a unique perspective on the guerrillas and on the Indian population. Will you come and be on the negotiating team?"

This was the confirmation I needed. I knew it would be dangerous, but I accepted the president's offer. I was going home.

Over the next few months, members of the peace commission met many times— officially and sometimes unofficially—and made significant progress. All but one of the major guerrilla organizations agreed to a cessation of violence. The holdout, ironically, was the more violent faction of the ELN.

There had been a split within the organization. Apparently my "missionary work" in the guerrilla camps had led to an upheaval in the ranks. At the time I was released, perhaps 60 percent of the two hundred or so guerrillas with whom I had come in contact had committed their lives to Christ. These new Christians had instigated a change in policy for all but the most militant members of the

> For the first time, the Indians were
> demonstrating a willingness and ability
> to work together and a determination to
> stand against the guerrillas and
> drug cartels.

ELN. They were now working to advance their goals through nonviolent means. It seemed that God's Spirit would not be constrained—even in the hearts of dedicated revolutionaries.

The result was a tentative but encouraging period of peace for northeastern Colombia, affecting the entire nation. We all hoped it would last.

During this same time, the Motilones organized a series of highly significant meetings with other tribal leaders representing fifty language groups—virtually all the Indians of Colombia. Together, they issued an ultimatum to the guerrilla forces and drug traffickers operating on their lands: "You have until December to clear out. If you don't go, you will be at war with all 500,000 of us."

The guerrillas and drug traffickers did not depart the area entirely as hoped. But this show of unity significantly strengthened the position of the tribes. For the first time, the Indians were demonstrating a willingness and ability to work together and a determination to stand against the guerrillas and drug cartels. Even though they coveted Indian territory, the guerrillas and drug lords, for the time being, mostly left the Indians alone. They did not want to risk open warfare with a capable and motivated opponent.

For many years, one of my dreams was that all of the Indian tribes would find a way to work together to secure their mutual futures. Ironically, my abduction provided the impetus for this to take place. While I was a prisoner, I never imagined that the tribes would rally together on my behalf. God showed me yet again how He was orchestrating events for His purposes, no matter how unfathomable they were at the time.

During the Indian meetings, tribal elders from across the nation also asked for help from the Motilones. They had come to respect the Motilones as examples of success and leaders for a unified and prosperous future for all the tribes. I was glad to see that these requests were not only for practical help in matters of medicine, agriculture, education, and economics, but also for information about the Spirit who guides the Motilones, Saymaydodji-ibateradacura.

The Motilones responded to this challenge with enthusiasm, forming thirty teams of three members each to reach out to the tribes throughout Colombia. It seemed that in my absence, the Motilones had grown more confident, more spiritually mature, and more capable than ever. I could not have been more satisfied.

Even in the darkest moments of my captivity, I never lost my faith that God remained with me and was still sovereign. I knew that His love for me would not wane, that I could trust Him to the end. The Motilones were equally faithful, believing that I was in God's hands and working with unwavering dedication to secure my release while simultaneously continuing the programs we had begun together.

While apart, both the Motilones and I had successfully sought to stay obedient to Saymaydodji-ibateradacura. Now we were together again, our faith strengthened anew, and our hearts content in Him as never before.

Chapter 14

Violence and Hope

At this moment we must wait on God. He will enlighten us. We will have His protection and refuge in our jungle, just as in the older days.

—ASERNDORA

Unfortunately, though I was highly pleased with and proud of the spiritual maturity demonstrated by the Motilones, I could not say the same for all other members of Colombian society. Not long after the truce negotiated by the peace commission in 1990, our "immature brothers"—many of the guerrillas, as well as the drug traffickers—were back to their old ways.

Even during the first days of relative calm, there were signs of trouble. The militant faction of the ELN, which had refused to participate in the peace process that led to a cessation of violence, remained involved in kidnappings, assassinations, and other terrorist acts on an almost daily basis. Early in 1990, they assassinated three mayors, a former governor, and a bishop in the Roman Catholic Church. They took four Americans hostage to protest President George H. W. Bush's visit to Colombia, though these captives were later released.

This violent faction of the ELN was also intent on eliminating me. I received several new threats on my life and orders to leave Colombia. I began to fear that I was being followed. At one point, I took a trip to a nearby town called Curumaní with several Motilones. Rather than make the trip by foot, we took a car. We decided to stop at a restaurant for something to eat and parked the car in a nearby parking garage. While we were inside the restaurant, a hand grenade was thrown into my car, and it exploded. The car and garage were destroyed, but thankfully no one was injured.

With incidents such as this occurring, I thought and prayed about whether it would be in everyone's best interest for me to depart permanently. Once again, however, my heart told me that I still belonged in Colombia. I felt I needed to continue the work God had called me to do and leave the outcome to Him.

Over the next two years, the peace talks gradually broke down. Rebel groups such as the FARC, ELN, and others increasingly returned to violent means to press their points. Public opinion shifted against the idea of dialogue with the insurgents; the government insisted that all violence end before talks could continue. At the same time the rebel guerrillas, who were dividing into small local interest groups, began pressuring the Motilones and other native peoples to become active combatants for their cause. This was completely contrary to the interest and mentality of most of the indigenous people.

There were hopeful signs in the midst of these disturbing events. I received numerous visits from the newly Christian revolutionaries I had met in the camps who had since split with the ELN to form their own movement. These young men were not only remaining faithful to their new commitment, but they were also growing in their knowledge of Scripture and taking the message of the gospel to guerrillas in other groups. Many of these latter guerrillas gave their lives to Jesus and left their organizations to join this new, Christ-centered movement.

Their departure came with considerable risk. The ELN pledge, for example, was, "Not one step backwards: liberation or death." The penalty for abandoning the cause was usually execution by firing squad. In May 1997, however, in an unprecedented action, the ELN released three hundred–plus Christians from their oath, describing them as "peacemakers." These former guerrillas were then granted amnesty for their past actions by the government and provided with the opportunity to reenter Colombian society—a remarkable turn of events.

Meanwhile, the government was also doing its best to shut down the country's drug trade. Several leaders of the Medellin and Cali drug cartels had been arrested or killed. By spraying enormous quantities of pesticides in southern Colombia, government forces had eradicated more than 123,000 acres of cocaine and heroine. The result, however, was that waves of people employed by or in support of the cartels moved to the borders of Motilone territory to establish new fields of drug corruption.

I was thrilled at this tangible proof that the
gospel was genuine and legitimate among
the Motilone body of believers. They had
reaffirmed the wisdom of trusting God
for the solution to their problems.

The Motilones were threatened by this undesired development and knew they would need God's wisdom to remain independent of the cartels' influence and protect their lands from intrusion. The tribal elders fasted and prayed, never doubting in His protection. In the months that followed, it sometimes seemed as if an invisible barrier had been placed between the Motilones and the drug forces. In the midst of tense circumstances, we were all grateful for a powerful sense of God's presence.

My gratitude grew even stronger a few weeks later.

In November 1997, more than two hundred fifty leaders from every tribal territory met in Tibú at the House of Twelve Cultures—*Axdobaringcayra*. They were refining tribal proposals on matters such as "territorial definitions," "health services," and "social goals of the indigenous peoples" to be made to the Colombian government at the invitation of the legislatures.

They also discussed concerns about violent incidents incited by guerrillas and drug traffickers encroaching on Motilone territory. The debate was unusually heated for the Motilones. An outspoken young man, Victor Asabana, proposed that the Motilones join forces with the guerrillas to protest against an indifferent government. Kaymiyokba wanted to align with the government because it had the stronger military force. Bobby Jr. and his grandfather, Aberdora, argued that the tribes should remain independent and autonomous.

Other young Motilones favored an aggressive response to snuff out any threats—a return to the past, when their warriors ruled the land with bow and arrow. But the elders reminded their youthful colleagues of a hard-earned lesson—that violence engenders violence.

It was a Motilone named Aserndora who stood and spoke most firmly and eloquently before the assembly.

"At this moment we must wait on God," he said. "He will enlighten us. He will guide us through the situation in which we find ourselves. We will have His protection and refuge in our jungle, just as in the older days." The other tribal elders soon voiced their agreement with Aserndora's words.

I was respectfully silent during the debate. In my heart, however, I was thrilled at this tangible proof that the gospel was genuine and legitimate among the Motilone body of believers. They had reaffirmed the wisdom of trusting God for the solution to their problems. The course they were choosing would take patience and restraint, but I was sure it would ultimately prove the most beneficial.

The chieftains commissioned me to write statements about what had been decided, which took another three days after the end of the meetings. Then I was ready to return to Bucaramanga by way of Cúcuta.

Early the next morning, a group of us piled into my faithful Toyota Land Cruiser, now seventeen years old. Cesar Abitubayeya, whose leg needed medical attention, sat in the front with me. Victor Asabana, his father, a woman named Atura, and her two children squeezed into the back. The drive to Cúcuta would be nearly four hours, most of it along muddy roads.

I was pleased with the results of our meetings, but also exhausted from the discussions and my efforts to summarize everything in writing. I looked forward to returning to the jungle.

We were about forty minutes into the journey when we came around a bend onto a clear stretch of road about one hundred yards long. The thick vegetation of the jungle lined the road on the left; on the right was a steep, fifty-foot drop into a river.

Suddenly, about twenty camouflaged guerrillas armed with rifles burst from the jungle onto the road, surrounding us. Some fired their weapons; a bullet ricocheted off my door.

"Stop!" several yelled. I jammed my foot on the brake. There was no chance of escape.

"Out of the car!"

I got out. Then, because Abitubayeya could barely walk, I helped him out as well. We were ordered to sit.

It was a well-planned ambush by the People's Liberation Army, or EPL. They had known I was at the meetings and were waiting for me. I was back in the hands of guerrillas.

The EPL was one of the revolutionary groups that Victor Asabana had forcefully advocated linking with just a few days before. Now Victor sat in the mud with the rest of us, looking miserable.

Two guerrillas approached. "Bruce Olson, you are being detained," one said to me. He tied my hands behind me while the other pointed his rifle at my head.

It had been just over eight years since my abduction by the ELN. I did not want to be a prisoner again. This time, I thought, they would certainly execute me.

The main group of guerrillas began arguing. Some wanted to go through our luggage, while the others were in a hurry to leave. As they talked, more vehicles arrived and were stopped—a car and bus in front of us, and a taxi and pickup truck behind us. There were fifteen or sixteen guerrillas in the middle of the roadway with us, plus another four revolutionaries stopping traffic at each end of the road. Our little stretch of highway was getting quite crowded.

The argument ended; it was time to leave. "You will come with us," said the guerrilla who had tied my hands. He ordered me into the passenger side of my Toyota while another guerrilla climbed behind the steering wheel.

It had been just over eight years since my abduction by the ELN. I did not want to be a prisoner again. This time, I thought, they would certainly execute me. But I was most distressed to see the looks on my companions' faces. I hated to leave them like this. What would happen to them?

My driver apparently had little experience with a stick shift. In attempting to turn around the Toyota, he backed up too far. The rear of the Land Cruiser slipped past the edge of the road—a few more inches and we would careen down the embankment into the river! The panicked driver threw the gearshift into first and slammed on the gas. We stopped moving backward, but there wasn't enough traction to move forward—one rear wheel was spinning uselessly, hanging over the precipice. We were in a precarious position.

At that moment, I heard the shouts of guerrillas: "Military! Military!"

Ahead of us, on the road from Cúcuta, I saw two cars with government police insignias appear behind the bus. I glanced at my captor in the driver's seat. He was staring at the police cars, eyes wide.

This was my chance. Clumsily, my hands still tied behind me, I opened my door and stumbled out of the Toyota. Everyone—guerrillas and the passengers in the stopped vehicles—ran for cover. Machine-gun fire erupted from the direction of the police cars. Bullets whistled by my head and slammed into the Land Cruiser.

I ran across the road to the jungle. There was Abitubayeya! I crouched next to him; he untied my hands. A grenade exploded on the road. I put an arm around Abitubayeya and helped him hop on his good leg deeper into the jungle.

The undergrowth was perhaps eight feet high. Thorns slashed our clothes and flesh as we stumbled forward, but we paid no attention. More grenades exploded behind us.

We came to a short but steep rise, followed by a small clearing. Inside it was the rest of our group: Victor, his father, and Atura and her children. I was relieved to realize no one was hurt.

Bullets have hit me in the leg and chest,
and I still have one lodged in my neck—
doctors have told me it's safer to leave it
there than try to remove it.

We were just high enough to see over the jungle undergrowth. Bullets were still flying on the road. Revolutionaries were loading wounded into the empty taxi. I counted the bodies of four guerrillas on the ground.

We moved deeper into the jungle.

We could hear the sounds of intense battle behind us. After about ten minutes, however, the noise died out. We stayed hidden for close to an hour, then crept back to the road.

Both the police and guerrillas had vanished. Bus passengers milled about, trying to decide what to do. The bus driver hooked a chain to the Toyota, still balanced on the edge of the cliff, and pulled it back to the road. My passengers got in, and we drove on to Cúcuta without further incident. Later, I learned that the police cars were a military escort for judges traveling to Tibú. Their arrival came at precisely the right moment for me to escape from the guerrillas.

I recalled Aserndora's last words at our meetings a few days before, two quotations from Scripture: "Be very careful, then, how you live—not as unwise but as wise, making the most of every opportunity, because the days are evil" (Eph. 5:15–16). And, "Even youths grow tired and weary, and young men stumble and fall; but those who hope in the LORD will renew their strength" (Isa. 40:30–31).

Aserndora, I thought, *is becoming a prophet among us.*

Our troubles with the guerrillas continued during the following years. In 1999, on the way to Bucaramanga, thirty university students and I were caught in a crossfire between guerrillas and military forces in the jungle. None in our group were hurt. The same thing happened four years later on the Rio de Oro. We were forced to hide out for three days in the jungle before continuing our journey. Later that year, I also survived another attempt on my life in the jungle.

I have been shot at—both intentionally and otherwise—so many times in Colombia that I have lost count. Bullets have hit me in the leg and chest, and

I still have one lodged in my neck—doctors have told me it's safer to leave it there than try to remove it. It is a constant reminder of the dangers around me.

During the nineties, as the guerrilla organizations struggled to keep their movements viable, they observed the success of the drug lords and the incredible profits available from growing and selling cocaine. Increasingly, the guerrillas compromised their revolutionary ideals and joined forces with the cartels and sympathetic colonists in the drug trade. Today, all of the significant guerrilla organizations operating in Colombia—the FARC, ELN, and EPL—finance their operations through drug profits. At the same time, paramilitary forces largely in support of the government and opposed to the guerrillas are also aligning with the drug lords when it is convenient.

All of these groups seek land for greater drug production and profits. This has led to frequent attempts to annex Motilone territory. In 2003, guerrillas seized four Motilone cooperatives and confiscated all goods and profits. They also took possession of the twelve-ton-capacity truck that was the only means of transporting chocolate harvests from the High Catatumbo region to Colombian markets. This severed the primary source of funding for many of our jungle health centers and schools, as well as scholarships for university students in the cities.

Yet for every crisis brought on by the escalation of violence that surrounds the Motilones, a solution has emerged. When the guerrillas took over the co-ops, tribal elders again concluded that "violence engenders violence." Instead of taking up bows and arrows, they responded with several days of fasting and prayer.

To the surprise of everyone but the Motilones, a communication misunderstanding among the guerrillas led to a battle between their own soldiers, which diminished their forces. Then the press announced an agreement to a unilateral cease-fire between the guerrilla groups and the government to explore a new peace proposal. The chocolate truck was returned, and we were able to reopen the cooperatives.

More recently, in November 2004, fourteen hundred guerrillas and drug traffickers turned in their weapons at the invitation of the government. They were granted amnesty for past actions and reinserted into Colombian society. It was a moment of hope amidst so much chaos and violence.

Today, that violence is still very much a part of life in Colombia and in the jungles in proximity to the Motilones. We must be extremely careful when we travel. Clashes between the guerrillas, drug traffickers, government forces, paramilitaries, and land settlers are commonplace. All too frequently, our once-pristine trails are littered with bodies and blood.

Clashes between the guerrillas,
drug traffickers, government forces,
paramilitaries, and land settlers are
commonplace. All too frequently,
our once-pristine trails are littered
with bodies and blood.

I do not know how or when peace will be achieved in the jungles and in Colombia. The antagonistic relationships between the groups are complex and longstanding. I worry about how the Motilones will maintain the cooperatives and their programs in medicine, agriculture, and education, as well as preserve their traditions and indeed their very lives, as these terrible conflicts continue.

And yet, I know what is possible. I have seen "immature brothers" turn their hearts toward Christ, lay down their arms, and start a new life of peace. And I have observed time and again how God has honored the efforts of the Motilones to "walk on His trail" and reject violence as a solution to problems. He has protected the Indians in ways that I never would have imagined, and He continues to protect them today. My fervent hope is that the Motilones will continue to place their trust in Christ—and that Jesus, in turn, will lead our nation to a transforming peace through the example of the Motilones, one heart at a time.

Chapter 15

Expanding Influence

Might our nation accept God's love provided in redemption and our society live in His hope in this twenty-first century.

—Julio

Over the years, a few critics have denounced me for encouraging changes that allowed outside influences to enter the jungle. These critics have painted the picture of an unstoppable tidal wave of modern decadence washing over a helpless, simpleminded native population.

This is an inaccurate and unfair portrait of the Motilones. The Indians I met in the early 1960s were a dignified, mature, and thoughtful people. It is true that they have allowed modern advances and conveniences into their lives—along with a few less desirable side effects. But it is also true that they have unleashed their own tidal wave, representing Motilone tradition, values, and faith, upon the region and even the world. Who can say, only a few years into the twenty-first century, which will have the greater influence?

When I conceived of a five-point plan of community development for the Motilones in the 1960s, I knew it would speed up the process of interaction with the outside world. I saw this process as inevitable. The land settlers were already moving into Motilone territory, and the oil companies and Colombian government were already looking for ways to communicate with the Indians. Interaction with the outside world had already begun, and the Motilones were at a disadvantage in this interaction. On top of this, the Motilones are insatiably curious. They wanted to know more about the outside world.

What I hoped to accomplish, then, within the limited means available to me was to give the Motilones tools to prosper in these increasing interactions. And as I look back on this effort, I am satisfied with what has taken place. Each point in the community development program has had a lasting, positive impact on the Motilone community. Equally exciting has been the impact of each, through the Motilones, on people *beyond* the jungles of the Catatumbo.

The reason for this expansion and success, in the words of Daniel Adjibacbayra, is that as the Motilones implement these programs they are guided by the compassion of their Creator: "Thanks to God's grace we walk by faith on the trail of life's experience toward the horizon, placing our steps in the footprints of Jesus Christ, Saymaydodji-ibateradacura." The Motilones desire to obey and emulate Jesus. They have not been content to keep their advances and profits to themselves. Instead, they are committed to sharing their abundance—and the good news of Jesus Himself—with the outside world.

The first objective of our program was to introduce medicines that would halt the spread of epidemics among the Indians. In 1963 we began to build the first clinic in Iquiacarora. By the beginning of 2003, this effort had grown to include the construction of twenty-three health centers strategically located throughout the jungle, including three beyond Motilone territory. Each had a concrete floor—more conducive to sanitary and stable health procedures—and medical equipment and supplies that previously had been unknown to the Motilones. All were equipped with at least one solar-powered computer. Several of these were able to take advantage of low-flying satellites to connect to the Internet. Communication between centers is also achieved by radio.

Each health center is staffed by two or three nurses and sometimes a physician, most often Motilone who have trained in Colombian universities. Under the sponsorship of the Motilones and myself, more than thirty-nine natives (Motilone and other tribes) have graduated as doctors after studying medicine or dentistry in the cities and then returned to serve in the jungle.

When I conceived of a five-point plan of community development for the Motilones in the 1960s, interaction with the outside world had already begun, and the Motilones were at a disadvantage in this interaction.

One of these is David Tegria Uncaria. The son of a medicine man of the U'Wa tribe, he is the eighth medical student to graduate from Bucaramanga's Industrial University of Santander (UIS) under our sponsorship. David attended one of our jungle schools in the isolated Cubara region before enrolling in high school study in Bucaramanga. At UIS, he researched parasite pathology and infections among the U'Wa in coordination with the UIS College of Medicine. His research will be invaluable to all the tribes in northeast Colombia.

These medically trained personnel have taken the offensive against certain health threats. For instance, they recently secured funds from an international consortium to organize and launch an anti-tuberculosis campaign. Motilone physicians and nurses are administering the three-year project in cooperation with tribal leaders.

The Motilones are also quick to lend their medical expertise during times of crisis. When a series of earthquakes devastated six municipalities in Central Colombia in early 1999, the Motilone assembly immediately sent four physicians and twenty nurses to the state of Quinido. The Motilone Co-op committed to funding expenses for half the team; Colombia's secretary of public health offered to cover the other half.

On arrival, the doctors set fractures, sutured wounds, and treated internal injuries as best as possible until patients could be evacuated by helicopter. The nurses, both men and women, spent most of their time pulling and digging out trapped victims from collapsed homes in the barrios. Over the next few days, Colombian and international relief workers arrived to help stabilize the chaotic scene. Some 2,000 people perished, and more than 180,000 were left homeless.

Later, Juancho Huamanae, one of the team members, was nearly in tears as he described the physical and emotional state of the victims.

"We worked twenty hours a day struggling to save lives," he said. "People were broken like buildings. It was as if survivors had been sucked into a mental vacuum of abandonment and hopelessness."

Juancho soon realized, however, that God has provided an opportunity in the midst of despair.

"Through medical procedures, the patients began to improve and their minds began to open to contemplating the future," Juancho said. "This presented for us a unique moment to share that just as Christ's body was broken for our healing and His blood shed for forgiveness of our sin, His resurrection provides redemption! Hundreds of our patients accepted Jesus into their lives and spiritually were reborn. Now they trust in His future!"

The second objective of our community development program was to begin agricultural efforts that would improve the diet of the Motilones, give them new foodstuff options during lean hunting seasons, and provide products for trade.

By 2003 we had established twenty-eight agricultural centers. Most of these were located within one hundred yards of a longhouse and in the same area as five or six small clearings, separated so that an infection in one plot could not wipe out an entire crop of corn, rice, beans, or vegetables.

Most of the centers also include small corrals and a stable for livestock such as cows, chickens, and pigs, which provide meat, milk products, and eggs. These efforts have led to some appreciated improvements for the Motilones. New mothers who cannot produce breast milk, for example, can give their babies decreamed milk from cattle. In addition, whey from butter contains natural bacteria that soothe the stomach and relieve diarrhea—a welcome change in any culture.

After years of struggle, negotiation, and coordination with the state and national legislatures, the president of Colombia signed an order in 1974 establishing approximately 320 square miles of Motilone territory—an area roughly one-third the size of Rhode Island—as an "Exclusive Motilone and Forest Reservation." It was in many ways a great triumph, as it finally provided legal protection for Motilone lands—the third goal of our program of community development.

Many tribal leaders were disappointed with the new law, however, in that the protected reservation did not also include the vast and fertile lowlands traditionally maintained by the Motilones. In the fifties, sixties, and seventies, land settlers looking for new opportunities and seeking to escape the cities—including some outlaws—flocked to this lowland territory. The government's response to this invasion was to legalize the territory for colonization under legislation titled National Agrarian Reform. Settlers received government-sponsored bank loans to stake out land. Then came slashing and burning of tropical jungle lowlands so that colonists could plant their own crops.

No one imagined that twenty-five years later, Motilone lawyers would be litigating their own claims on these lowlands.

In 1996, National Agrarian Reform legislation was again enacted—only this time, through government purchase of land from the settlers, most of the lowlands were legally returned to the Motilones.

The Motilones desire to obey and emulate
Jesus. They have not been content to keep
their advances and profits to themselves.
Instead, they are committed to sharing
their abundance—and the good news of
Jesus Himself—with the outside world.

When the Motilones discovered the power of the written word, their thirst for knowledge was awakened. This led to the fourth point in our development program: to establish bilingual schools in the jungle for the Motilones. The first bilingual school began in 1966. By early 2003, we were operating twenty-eight schools certified by the government and available to the Motilones, the other eighteen tribes in Northeast Colombia, and neighboring land settlers. These were led by the Motilones themselves, who had been trained as instructors, and by Colombian teachers I hired to teach Spanish. Initial funding for the instructors and materials came from the cooperatives and myself, but eventually the government paid the salaries of the Colombian teachers.

Many of our jungle school graduates continued their studies in the cities. In recent years we have had as many as forty-eight indigenous students enrolled at one time in Colombian universities. We have graduated more than fifty professionals—attorneys, accountants, translators, Bible scholars, forest rangers, agronomists, teachers, linguists—and thirty-nine physicians from the universities, while over four hundred students have earned technical apprentice degrees or completed their final two years of high school (equivalent to the first two years of college in the United States) at city institutions. Nearly all received full or partial scholarships from the Motilones or my own contributions.

To house students in Bucaramanga, we adjoined four apartments on the top floor of a condominium complex that I had purchased. The interior was rearranged and divided to accommodate the needs of the students; we established a dormitory, lounge, study hall, expanded kitchen, and dining area. I also built twelve computers for the students, each connected to the Internet. The setting was comfortable and decidedly Western, but the students were reminded of home when they saw their handcrafted hammocks, which had been transported from the jungle and placed in their rooms alongside the bunk beds. The scholarships funded by the Motilones and myself covered all costs for room and board, food, uniforms, books, and supplies.

Of the more than four hundred students who have pursued coursework in the cities, all are back among their respective communities sharing their newly acquired knowledge and expertise under the wisdom and direction of the tribal chieftains and elders. This is one of the most satisfying developments that I have observed in my years in the Catatumbo. It is a testament to each Motilone's commitment to his or her community. They have learned to incorporate the advantages of the modern world into their traditions and culture without losing their identities as native peoples of Colombia.

Julio is just one example of these students. Julio graduated from a jungle school in 1991. We provided a full scholarship for him to attend high school in Bucaramanga, where he graduated with honors. He then enrolled in the journalism program at Autonomous University of Bucaramanga (UNAB).

During a vacation from university study, Julio was walking along a jungle trail near his family's home when he saw the glint of an object in the brush. It was a dirty, battered mirror that someone had discarded along the trail.

Julio was filled with disgust. Who could be so thoughtless as to litter the pristine jungle floor with rubbish from the outside world? He knew just what to do. He would make his own protest of this irresponsible attitude by publishing a photograph of the mirror carelessly left in the jungle.

Then he peered at the mirror in his hand. He could barely make out his reflection through the grime. A Scripture passage came to mind: "Now we see but a poor reflection as in a mirror; then we shall see face to face. Now I know in part; then I shall know fully, even as I am fully known" (1 Cor. 13:12).

Such are our lives without Saymaydodji-ibateradacura, Julio thought. *Just a dim reflection of hope.*

When the Motilones discovered the power of the written word, their thirst for knowledge was awakened.

Julio changed his mind. He would still take a photo of the mirror, but his own image would be visible within the borders of the grubby glass. It would be a self-portrait inspired by the words of Scripture. He would call it "A Poor Reflection."

This image was honored as "Best Photograph 2001" by the Latin American Federation of Journalism. When Julio accepted the award in front of UNAB faculty and students, he closed his remarks by reading from Scripture in the Barí language: "'And now these three remain: faith, hope and love. But the greatest of these is love' (1 Cor. 13:13). Might our nation accept God's love provided in redemption and our society live in His hope in this twenty-first century."

The Colombian people, long plagued by division and violence, long for peace, a reconciled society, and the renewal of social values. Julio's words struck a chord. After a few moments of respectful silence, the audience gave him a standing ovation.

Today Julio is a reporter writing about the Motilones and their values from their own perspective, but he does not publish under his own name. The Motilones have determined, and wisely so, that if one person is singled out, he can be killed, so everything Julio writes is published in the name of the Motilones, or Barí, as they call themselves.

Julio's newly developed skills will benefit the Motilones for years to come. Yet the application of his talents and thoughtful commitment to his faith have already had an impact far beyond the jungle trails of Motilone territory.

The last objective of our community development program was to establish an economic system that would give the Motilones the ability to purchase medicine and other valuable tools, pay for educational materials, and journey to and trade with the outside world. This led to the birth of the cooperatives and our success in growing cocoa beans that were sold and converted into chocolate.

By the end of 2003, despite the seizure of four cooperatives by guerrillas, we were operating twenty-two co-ops, most of them in Motilone territory. Nearly half of the membership of the major cooperatives is made up of Spanish-speaking nationals and colonists who have asked to join. The Motilones continue to manage the co-ops, however, and still allocate funds for social needs. Following the example of the Indians, the Colombian government has at times matched Motilone contributions to these social concerns.

The Colombian people, long plagued
by division and violence,
long for peace, a reconciled society,
and the renewal of social values.

In each of these areas of community development, the Motilones have achieved a sustained level of success. More than ever before, they are healthy and financially independent. They have learned how to dialogue as equals with official representatives of the Colombian government and leaders from around the world. They have the means and skills to forge a future of their choosing.

The thread that ties these achievements together, however, has nothing to do with programs or worldly progress. It is the Motilones' faith in a God who in all things "works for the good of those who love him" (Rom. 8:28) that guides and sustains them. They are a spiritual people who have discovered the saving redemption of Jesus. Perhaps 90 percent of the five thousand Motilones living in the jungle today have been baptized in the name of Saymaydodji-ibateradacura.

Moreover, the Motilones wholeheartedly embrace the responsibility of sharing their faith with other tribes and other nations. They are continually alert to opportunities to be used by Him.

One such opportunity came a few years ago. A Motilone medical student had been assigned to complete a portion of his internship at a hospital in the city of Arauca, southeast of Motilone territory. He had been there only a month when an influential and anxious chieftain from the remote Guahibo tribe arrived in the emergency ward.

The chieftain was accompanied by three equally anxious tribal leaders. It was extremely rare for these Indians to journey from the jungle to the city, but they were desperate. The chieftain was dying. Traditional Guahibo herbs and incantations had been ineffective.

The Motilone med student attended to the chieftain. When the Guahibo leader saw who was caring for him, he began to relax. He recognized the face. Several years before, when this Motilone was a high school student in the jungle, he and several other members of a Motilone missionary team had shared about the good news during a visit with the Guahibo. The Guahibo had shown little interest in the message but had been gracious to the messengers.

The chieftain's medical condition was complex. To obtain an accurate diagnosis, he needed a fourteen-hour ambulance trip to the more sophisticated general hospital in Cúcuta. The director of Indian affairs based in Cúcuta stepped in to make arrangements and was at the hospital to greet the chieftain. Once again, the Guahibo's anxieties were relieved. He had met the director previously as well—another Motilone!

The ailing chieftain told his Guahibo companions that it was more than just coincidence that he kept finding himself in the care of the Motilones. He had had a vision before the journey to the city. In it, the "Great Spirit" had promised to provide friends to prepare the chieftain for recovery.

The lab results in Cúcuta offered little reason for hope, however. The chieftain had a chronic brain condition induced by malaria and a severe coronary affliction. He was not expected to survive.

Another Motilone—Odo, Bobby's adopted son—happened to be in Cúcuta on business as a representative of the tribe. The director of Indian affairs invited him to visit the chieftain at the hospital.

Odo did not know this Guahibo who was so seriously ill and far from his home and family, but at his bedside Odo sensed the restlessness in the chieftain's spirit. Tenderly he anointed the chieftain with oil. Both the med student and the director of Indian affairs crossed their arms over their foreheads in the Motilone expression of reverence.

The chieftain trusted in the goodwill of the Motilones and in the power of the oil. This "potion," he felt, was the reason for his vision and the key to his recovery.

Odo then prayed for the chieftain, asking for healing and declaring that the "source of all strength" was the resurrection of Saymaydodji-ibateradacura, Jesus Christ.

The chieftain was surprised and confused. Odo had not even mentioned the oil. What was this strength he spoke of? Then the other Guahibo leaders reminded the chieftain of the "foolish" words the Motilone missionaries had communicated during their visit years before. The chieftain listened intently as his companions discussed the nearly forgotten message of Saymaydodji-ibateradacura.

Suddenly, the chieftain broke down. Tears of joy filled his eyes. This was the real reason for the vision—to introduce him to the true Great Spirit, Saymaydodji-ibateradacura. There in the hospital room, the chieftain surrendered his frail life to Jesus. Again Odo prayed, this time thanking Jesus that a new brother had begun his journey on the trail of life's experiences.

The thread that ties these achievements together, however, has nothing to do with programs or worldly progress. It is the Motilones' faith in God.

A few weeks later, the chieftain was discharged from the hospital, completely recovered and with a new message of hope for his people. Through this unanticipated meeting, the efforts of Motilone missionaries years ago linked with a fresh opportunity provided by God to deliver the good news of Jesus to their neighbors in the tribal areas surrounding Motilone territory. It was just one more sign of the spreading influence of the Motilones.

The impact of the Motilone has not only been limited to the indigenous peoples and citizens of Colombia. In 1992, for example, Fidel Waysersera and Roberto Dacsarara, the first Motilones to graduate from national universities, represented Colombia as delegates to the United Nations Congress on Environment and Development. Representatives from 172 nations and every continent in the world attended the Earth Summit, as it was informally known, in Rio de Janeiro.

At the two-week conference, the Motilone pair encountered an astonishing array of people and cultures. Among these were Brazilian jungle tribal peoples. The tribal peoples were adorned in parrot feathers and loincloths, their bodies decorated in natural vegetable paints in red and blue hues. They put on an impressive dance show, especially delighting photographers and tourists.

A newspaper reporter, noting Dacsarara's suit and tie and identification tag as a Motilone Indian of Colombia, inquired, "Where are *your* feathers?"

Dacsarara thought for a moment before answering in Spanish. "I come to discuss and champion indigenous land rights as contemplated by Western law. And I come to declare solidarity with the protection of the environment, the concern of this Earth Summit. I left my feathers and loincloth hanging in the rafters of our palm-thatched community house. When I return to the jungle, I'll enjoy donning them and dancing with the wind blowing through my hair. But now I come to the city; I dress as everyone else.

"We have come," he said, gesturing at Waysersera nearby, who was also wearing a suit, "to look for solutions to problems that bring suffering to Planet Earth."

Later, the Brazilian natives were told of Dacsarara's comments. They spent the rest of the conference dressed in Western-style slacks and shirts, intent on learning from the Motilones how they might protect their habitats from the encroachment of land settlers and protect the health of their communities by applying basic concepts in preventive medicine. They discovered that the Motilones were models of progress in these areas.

Two months later, several of the Brazilian natives traveled to Colombia to visit the Motilones and see these programs for themselves. They were aware that throughout South America's history, many native peoples have been overwhelmed by contact with the modern, Western world. Many of these are discouraged and see no future for their tribes. The Brazilian natives reported, however, how impressed they were with the self-esteem displayed by the Motilones. They said the Motilones had made a dynamic transition from monolingual, monocultural, traditional jungle dwellers to catalysts of progressive ideas and effective leaders for progress in their region and nation.

These meetings were the beginning of dialogues between the Motilones and their new friends in Brazil. It provided them the opportunity to plant the seeds of their faith in a new culture and nation, seeds that they yet believe will grow and flourish in the years ahead.

It gives me great fulfillment to know that my adopted family has taken to heart the words of Jesus—to "go and make disciples of all nations" (Matt. 28:19). Their spiritual influence on the outside world is clearly more pronounced than the reverse. And it has had its effect on me as well. The Motilones bring a confidence, maturity, and enthusiasm to their faith that has inspired me many times. They are at peace with God. Though I, the missionary, may have introduced them to a personal relationship with Jesus, I find that after all these years, they are yet instructing me in matters of the Spirit.

When the apostle Paul wrote to the Colossians in the first century A.D., he might as well have been summarizing my own feelings toward the Motilones two thousand years later:

> We always thank God, the Father of our Lord Jesus Christ, when we pray for you, because we have heard of your faith in Christ Jesus and of the love you have for all the saints—the faith and love that spring from the hope that is stored up for you in heaven and that you have already heard about in the word of truth, the gospel that has come to you. All over the world this gospel is bearing fruit and growing, just as it has been doing among you since the day you heard it and understood God's grace in all its truth.
>
> —Colossians 1:3–6

Chapter 16

Transition to the Twenty-first Century

We must understand who we are as Colombians in the twenty-first century, how we can defend our land through legislation, and how we can reconcile with our young people—of whom I am one—so that we can recover the beliefs and values of our grandparents.

—CESAR ABITUBAYEYA

As the Motilones make the transition from tribal communities sheltered from modern influences to a people coming into frequent contact with "advanced" societies, they inevitably experience challenges. New opportunities in education and careers, technological and medical enhancements, and freedoms promoted by Western culture also mean many more choices. With so many alternatives before them, the Motilones need the presence and insight of Christ to guide them more than ever before.

I especially see this need among the second and third generations of Motilones who are walking on the trail of Saymaydodji-ibateradacura. The men and women of Bobaríshora's generation grew up with the traditions of their elders. They learned to respect the spirit of the cave, of the wind, of the plants, and of the jungle that surround them. In ways that only they fully comprehend, the habitat that God has entrusted to the Motilones is a spiritual, living place that whispers wisdom to them from across the ages.

Like their parents, "second-generation" Motilones such as Odo, Bobby Jr., and Cuadudura grew up with this appreciation for the traditions of their elders. In addition, they have studied in the cities and experienced what the larger world can offer. Yet, in most cases, they retain a healthy wariness of the influence of outside forces. They have seen or been touched by many examples of contact with "civilized" society that have brought on difficulty or tragedy, not least the murder of Bobby.

For third-generation Motilones, however, the situation is more complex. They are being raised in an environment where the enticements of Western culture are more apparent and obtainable. Many of the Motilones, for example, now choose to live outside of traditional longhouses in smaller homes constructed of wood or cement blocks that are placed around the perimeter of the longhouses. Many of these homes contain modern conveniences purchased through the cooperatives.

I do not begrudge the Motilones for taking advantage of these opportunities. They certainly have the right to choose a lifestyle that is more comfortable. But especially in the case of the third-generation Motilones, I fear that they do not always understand the consequences of their choices. Other jungle tribes in Colombia have embraced Western culture and discovered "side effects" such as problems with alcohol and drug use. I do not want to see this happen to the Motilones. I pray that it will not.

I am also troubled at times by the attitude of some Motilones toward our violent neighbors, members of the drug cartels, guerrilla organizations, and paramilitaries. The Motilones believe that to understand how to hunt a monkey or a parrot, you must go into the jungle and live with the monkeys and parrots. By spending time with them, you discover their strengths and weaknesses. This is how you learn to sing like a monkey or call like a parrot so that they will come to you on a hunt. Some are applying this same approach to the drug traffickers and guerrilla fighters. They believe that to understand the problems among these groups, they must be in dialogue with them and live near them.

It is a dangerous philosophy. Of course, 90 percent of the comments I hear from those attempting to dialogue with left-wing groups are negative. But I observe too many Motilones not just learning about the weaknesses of our neighbors, but also acquiring them. For instance, I know of Indians growing cocaine in their fields and then pulling out the plants to show to the government so they can be paid for "eradicating" cocaine. Then they use the funds, which come from the Colombian and U.S. governments, to buy crops to grow more cocaine. Most Motilones decry this procedure as illegal and immoral, but it is an example of the challenges Colombia's indigenous peoples are contending with today.

> The Motilones certainly have the right to choose a lifestyle that is more comfortable. But especially in the case of the third-generation Motilones, I fear that they do not always understand the consequences of their choices.

Because I strongly believe that the Motilones should maintain their traditions and culture, my ideas are not always compatible with those of the Indians, particularly the youth who are just now coming into positions of leadership and influence. I must respect their feelings. When I am with them, I am less vocal about my opinions. We talk about family matters and other less controversial topics. When I am in the jungle, I usually stay with the tribal elders. They are the ones with a deeper understanding of the complexities of merging the old and new, as well as the people with the responsibility for seeing this carried out, and so we discuss these issues. They are my contemporaries, and I am more comfortable with them. When I first came to the Motilones as a young man, it was the elders who were most suspicious of me and the youth who were most receptive. Today I am in my mid-sixties, and it is the elders who most appreciate whatever wisdom God would share through me.

The Motilones do not always agree among themselves either. It is a turbulent and exciting time, but I am encouraged that they continue to rely on the guidance of Christ. My hope is that God will enlighten them so that they can continue to walk on the path that Saymaydodji-ibateradacura has set before them.

The story of Cesar Abitubayeya may better illustrate the challenge—and the hope—that the Motilones have as they transition into the twenty-first century. Cesar, from the remote Sacacdú community along the river that gives birth to the Rio de Oro, is a third-generation believer among the Motilones. His grandparents were among the early Motilone followers of Christ. When he was nine, however, Cesar left his village to live with a family of Colombian colonists. They put him to work, introduced him to a materialistic lifestyle, and taught him to look down on his Motilone brothers and sisters.

Cesar eventually returned to Sacacdú, but he had little feeling for his community and no use for the traditions of his elders. He even forced some of the Motilones off their land so that colonists could move in. I had known him since he was a little boy, and after he came back to Sacacdú, he tried to get me to help him purchase Western conveniences such as a television. I felt it would be a mistake, as well as a waste of my time and funds, so I repeatedly turned him down. Cesar became cool and distant toward me.

About nine years ago, when Cesar was twenty-four, he went to a clearing near the Catatumbo River that he had made for growing corn and rice. While he was bent down inspecting the soil, an enormous tree that had been weakened by fire suddenly gave way. Cesar attempted to scramble to safety but was a moment too late—the trunk fell on his left leg, crushing it.

Cesar was eventually sent to a hospital in Cúcuta, where a doctor examined the leg and put it in a cast. But something was not right, and Cesar knew it. Which led to the surprise phone call I received a few days later.

"Yado," Cesar said after explaining what had happened, "the pain is terrible. I know something is wrong. I am going to lose my leg." I told him that since a doctor had treated him and put on a cast, he would soon be all right. But Cesar could not be consoled. Finally I asked, "Well, what do you want from me?"

There was a pause. "I want you to come to Cúcuta," Cesar said in a low voice. "I want you to help me."

I was touched. I knew how difficult it was for him to ask for my help. I agreed to leave within the hour.

It was an eight-hour drive through the Andes Mountains to Cúcuta. I found Cesar in a tiny, tin-roof shanty, miserable in the 110-degree heat, his leg propped up on a tree stump. Sweat covered his forehead below his thick, black hair. Still, I felt the need to test him. I wanted to make sure his plea for assistance was genuine. "Oh, you have a beautiful white cast," I said. "It's lovely. You must feel better now."

He stared at me. "Just because the cast is white and the leg is elevated doesn't mean it's all right," he said. "It hurts. Something's wrong."

I tested him again. "Look at all the colonists who have signed your cast," I said. "You have many friends. You don't need me."

Again, Cesar swallowed his pride. "I want *you* to help me."

This time I knew for certain. Cesar truly feared that he would lose his leg, and he believed I was his best hope. I said I would help and care for him, provided he would live under my conditions. Cesar agreed. I made arrangements with a doctor friend in Bucaramanga. The doctor reluctantly agreed to postpone a vacation if we could be at his clinic the next day.

After taking x-rays, my friend said the previous doctor had done nothing for Cesar but put on a cast. "His leg is totally crushed," my friend said. "I don't know if we can save the leg." But he was willing to try. What was anticipated as a four- or five-hour operation turned into fourteen hours of surgery. The doctor reconstructed bone, inserted pins, put in wire meshing to hold bone fragments together, and scraped away the beginnings of gangrene. "Never have I worked so hard in my life," he said when it was over. "But I think something miraculous is going to happen. I don't think he will lose the leg."

The next day at the clinic, Cesar was in agonizing pain. "I feel as if a bus has parked on my body," he said through tears. "I ache."

I felt sympathy for Cesar. I knew he was suffering. I remembered my own suffering at the hands of the guerrillas after my abduction. Now I felt a bond with this troubled young man who had called for my help.

I recalled how I had survived the trauma of diverticulitis, internal bleeding, and being shackled for weeks to a tree: my spirit had left my physical body and risen into the jungle canopy. I had been able to look down on my body from far above and leave my pain behind. It was a spiritual experience that the Motilone elders understood and knew well. I shared this with Cesar in the language and custom of his people.

"You know I don't believe in the traditions of my people," he said, his face still contorted with pain. "I am a modern man, a progressive."

"Perhaps," I said, "this is a moment to reflect back to the values of your grandparents. You may find an inner strength. If you ask God to bring strength and understanding, I believe He will provide it."

Cesar turned away and seemed to stare at a picture on the wall. But after a few minutes, his breathing grew deeper and his body went limp. A few minutes later, he spoke to me in a calm voice: "I no longer feel pain. I can watch what's in the room. I am no longer in my body." I could hear the surprise and relief in his voice, and I understood.

Cesar had almost no money, so I paid for his hospital stay. When I talked to my friend the doctor about paying the surgeon's fee, he shook his head. "Bruce, I'm not going to charge you," he said. "I think God has touched this boy. He is going to do something special with him."

Cesar stayed with me after he was discharged from the clinic. After two and a half weeks, I removed the stitches myself. He faced six or seven months of recovery and physical therapy, but the leg looked marvelous.

I felt sympathy for Cesar. I knew he was suffering. I remembered my own suffering at the hands of the guerrillas after my abduction. Now I felt a bond with this troubled young man who had called for my help.

The experience of the injury, the operation, and his ability to survive the pain by reviving a Motilone tradition changed Cesar. He gave up the feeling that he deserved a better life and that he was "above" his people. With my encouragement, he decided to renew his schooling. Though he had never finished high school, he caught up quickly, earning credit for three years of study in just two.

One day, not long before Cesar finished his high school coursework, he and I sat on the balcony of my apartment in Bucaramanga and watched the passersby. I was pleased to see the change in Cesar and proud of how hard he had worked on his studies. Now I wondered what would come next.

"Cesar, your leg is healed and your studies are nearly complete," I said. "What are you going to do with your life?"

He took a deep breath. "I think something has happened to me, something in my spirit," he said quietly. "I'm grateful to my grandparents that they didn't abandon me in my sufferings. And I'm grateful to you. If not for you, I wouldn't be alive."

"Many people worked together to save your life," I said.

Cesar thought about that. "I owe society something," he said at last. "I want to go to university. I want to study law."

It was an ambitious goal for someone of his age and background, and I had my doubts that it was possible. But I spoke to the president of Free University in Cúcuta, and he agreed to give Cesar a chance. And Cesar made the most of it. Five years later, he earned his law degree with high marks.

Today, Cesar Abitubayeya is an attorney who lives in the jungle with the Motilones. He has the respect both of his peers at the university and in law circles, and of the Motilone elders and community members. He remains in many ways a "modern man," but he has reconciled with the traditional values of his grandparents. Where there is conflict between Motilone tradition and modern law, he looks for ways to reconcile these differences as well. Where once he gave away Motilone territory to outsiders out of shame for his people, now he works with Motilone elders and through the Colombian judicial system to protect and recover land for the Indians.

Recently, more than twelve hundred Motilones gathered in Bridicayra for a council of chieftains to discuss the violence and other problems plaguing their tribe. After listening to hours of testimony, Cesar stood so that his own voice could be heard. "We must understand who we are as Colombians in the twenty-first century," he said, "how we can defend our land through legislation, and how we can reconcile with our young people—of whom I am one—so that we can recover the beliefs and values of our grandparents that we have ignored. We must

I have seen many third-generation
Motilones embrace the culture and
traditions of their ancestors. I hope it
is the beginning of a trend.

ask the elders to share with us so that we can learn the spirit of the cave and the wind and the plants. These are the things God gave to our people when we did not have His Word."

God has had mercy on Cesar. It was not right for Cesar to abandon the traditions of his people. It also was not right for me to test him so harshly when he needed my help. But God brought us together and achieved a remarkable transformation in Cesar that is now affecting the Motilones in profound ways. I believe that God, in His loving way, is continuing to bring people together and bridge gaps to accomplish His purposes for the Motilones.

The pendulum may already be swinging back. I have seen many third-generation Motilones embrace the culture and traditions of their ancestors. I hope it is the beginning of a trend. I hope that the young people, along with the university students and graduates, as well as the older community members, will all trust and respect the wisdom and values of the tribal elders—the leaders who must guide their people into a modern world while still respecting and preserving the messages of the whispering winds, the echo of the caves, and the voices of the trees.

Another sign that this may indeed be happening was the publication in 2003 of *Ichidji ya ababi: Algo nuestro, así somos los Barí* [All of Us: Something About Who We Are, the Barí], a book about the Motilones—who call themselves *Barí*—written by the Indians themselves.[1] Twenty-three tribal communities representing more than five thousand people joined in the effort. It described their rich history; their evaluation of Motilone culture, values, economy, and habitat; and their goals for the future. One Colombian newspaper editorial, commenting on the book, stated, "If we want to know about peace, self-respect and coexistence, here's a challenge and example to emulate—the Barí."

Near the end of *Ichidji ya ababi*, the authors wrote about their aims in the arena of education:

> We the Barí want our schools to cultivate our traditional values, to foster
> sports championships in hunting and fishing; to teach students little by
> little how to organize and operate a horticulture program that is taught

in the land of the Barí; we want our wise men and elders integrated, so that our history is not forgotten. We want ethnic schools, while not forgetting that Barí will be the primary language.

We also hope for the development of cultural activities that feature our artists, songs, and traditions that will facilitate our expression of our vision of the life of our existing community....

We want to know education experiences that other towns have had because we want to learn, evaluate, and build our own proper path.

The Motilones are doing exactly that—learning, evaluating, and forging a path to their future. No doubt they will stumble at times along their journey, but I am encouraged that with eyes fixed on the horizon and hearts set on Christ, they will discover the fulfillment of dreams I cannot even imagine.

Chapter 17

Content With the Future

Yado, wherever you die, I will recover your body and take you back to the jungle. Then we will wrap you in a hammock and lift you into the jungle canopy, so that you can travel beyond the horizon as one of us.

—ARAYBACHIRA

Just as the Motilones have entered a time of transition with the arrival of the twenty-first century, so too am I in a period of transition. When I walked into the jungle more than forty years ago, I sensed a clear calling from God. My mission was to find the Motilone Indians, get to know them and their language and customs, and introduce them, if I could, to the saving grace of Jesus Christ. I did not go for the adventure. I went in response to what I felt was God's will for my life and to find peace in my heart. But at times I have wondered if the Motilones are truly glad about the changes that have taken place over the last four decades.

Last year, while bathing in the river with some of the Motilone men, I felt someone thrust a finger into the scar in my thigh—my permanent reminder of the arrow that had pierced me upon my first encounter with the Motilones many years ago. I turned to see Bisandora, a Motilone I had known since those early days, pointing to the scar.

"I am the one who shot you," he stated.

The confession came as a surprise to me. I suddenly realized that in more than forty years I had never once wondered which warrior had wounded me that day. But Bisandora's next statement surprised me even more.

"If I had not shot you, you would have run away from us."

I could see that it was not an admission of guilt; it was an announcement of honor.

On that long ago day, he had shot an arrow into my leg to prevent me from *invading* Motilone territory. But now at age eighty-six, looking back on the event, he realized that his shot had prevented me from *leaving* them, and he was proud to have been the one who had made that possible. His changed perspective on the outcome of my arrival was a welcome reassurance at a time doubts were rising within me.

Over the years, these fleeting doubts and questions had always been answered by an inner peace that God was not finished with His plan for me in South America. In 1977, when Andres Küng interviewed me for his book *Bruce Olson: Missionary or Colonizer?*, he asked me how long I planned to remain among the Motilones and recorded my answer.

> God has given me an assignment and He'll let me know when it is completed. I don't want to say that I am God-like or irreplaceable, only that I feel a power within me that decides these things for me. That power from above will show me and the Motilones the way in the future. When God wants me to, I am ready to pack up my bags and move on, as poor as when I arrived.[1]

Several years earlier, on July 20, 1969, as I lay in my hammock in the heart of a South American jungle, bows and arrows for killing the next day's dinner nearby, I listened to a broadcast on my transistor radio. An announcer was describing a pinnacle of scientific achievement, mankind's first walk on the moon. As I heard the news, part of me wanted to pack up and go where cars and planes and streetcars ruled instead of panthers and wild boars. But I knew there was a purpose for my presence in the jungle, and I was content to fulfill that purpose.

As I write this book today, however, my feelings are not so easily defined. I am sensing the leading of the Lord to begin my walk out of the jungle. The Motilones are free, independent thinkers. I have helped them acquire the tools they need—medicine, agriculture, education, an economy—to chart their own course. I am always willing to instruct or advise when asked, but now I must step back and trust the Holy Spirit to guide my friends and lead them to the truth. Sometimes they make decisions I do not agree with. But this is their time to make their own choices, as well as to learn from their mistakes, and I must respect that.

When I was abducted by the ELN in 1988, I believed I had a cause to die for—protection of the Motilones' God-given territory, their integrity as an autonomous group and as the original inhabitants of their nation. Then, outside forces threatened to overwhelm them. But today, the circumstances are changing. The Motilones have a much greater understanding of the influences that surround them, and in some cases they are inviting this influence into their communities. They are determining their own future.

In the last year or two, as I have traveled in the United States and elsewhere, God has confirmed in my heart that I can be absent from my adopted family and not be estranged. I still long to be with them, and they continue to welcome me with smiles, songs, endearing gestures of hands on my shoulders, and informal "hammock conversations" into the wee hours of the morning whenever I return. But my place in the jungle is not as important as it once was. I am loved just as much, but needed less. This is as it should be.

I suppose I feel something like a parent feels when watching a son or daughter leave home: proud, hopeful, anxious, wondering if I could have done something more or better or differently. And praying always for God's blessing and protection for them.

Have I done what I came to the jungle to do? Yes. I never thought I would be able to say that, but today I realize it is so. I have seen the gospel disseminated among the tribes. I have helped the Motilones translate the New Testament into their language and assisted in other Bible translations in other Indian languages. I have worked with the Indians to create more than twenty books in tribal languages. I have taught creative writing so that the Motilones and other tribes can relate their histories from their own point of view. I have helped them establish an economic system so that they can trade with the outside world. I have supported the Indians' desire for education so that they can realize a better understanding of the complex issues facing their region and negotiate with other citizens of Colombia and Venezuela on an equal level. I have worked to help them establish legal claims on the land that has been theirs for centuries. I have seen the country's indigenous people involved in politics and serving in local and national governments for the first time in their history.

An outside observer, commenting on all that has transpired, might very well describe it as a miracle. And perhaps it is, though the Motilones would never see it that way. They would say only that, "When you follow in the footsteps of Saymaydodji-ibateradacura, what else would you expect?" I am inclined to agree with them.

> I feel something like a parent feels when watching a son or daughter leave home: proud, hopeful, anxious, wondering if I could have done something more or better or differently.

The Motilone women are known for their ability to weave with simple looms, producing loincloths and canvas skirts that may be both functional and beautiful. Sometimes, as when Atacadara allowed the "mistakes" produced by her young daughter's fingers to remain in the pattern, they accomplish even more. Their work describes the legacy of a people, showing how lives intersect. It tells a story of love.

I too am a weaver. I have enjoyed the feel of material between my fingers since I was a boy, and I still produce textiles on occasion for my friend in Texas. But I am also a weaver in another way. Whatever talent God has given me to serve Him and the Motilones includes some ability to mold circumstances and people in a manner that can lead to His solutions. My "art," if it could be called that, has been to live among the Indians so that together we could weave a tapestry that is pleasing to God. Like Atacadara, He has allowed the efforts of my "fingers" to remain in the pattern. It has produced a colorful, rich work filled with history, warm relationships, and tales of lives opening up to the Savior. It too is a story of love.

Of course, there has also been heartache. Christ suffered for us on the cross, and I have come to understand that in God's wisdom it is necessary for us to suffer. The apostle Paul spoke of this: "I want to know Christ and the power of his resurrection and the fellowship of sharing in his sufferings" (Phil. 3:10). It is an experience that allows us to know Christ intimately. Bobby understood this. I have found the same concept elsewhere in Scripture, and I have encountered it in my own life. I accept it.

I do not mean to say that acceptance is an answer for loss. I agonized over the deaths of Bobby and Gloria. In Bobby's case, I could at least see how his death brought him the fulfillment he sought, to become like Christ. But with Gloria, I could not understand why her life had to end. She was so young, and to die in a car accident seemed so pointless.

At other times I have been near death, either at the hands of ELN thugs, or when I was battling Chagas' disease, or when I was shot in the neck, chest, and legs. It is terrible to suffer, and I certainly would not seek it out. But when it comes, I trust in God's sovereignty. He does not toy with our lives. I have learned not to judge Him. We tend to accuse Him when awful things happen. But we are His creations, fully dependent on Him. It is not our place to judge. This, I think, is one of the great discoveries I have made during my life with the Motilones. I wonder if I would have realized it had I ignored God's prompting and spent my life in Minnesota. I have learned much from my days in the jungle. I have shared the gospel with the Motilones, and they have shared the practicality of the gospel with me.

A friend said to me recently, "Bruce, you didn't need to be in the jungle all this time. You've stayed on too long." I disagree. I have kept my word and my commitments. I have fulfilled God's call on my life as a missionary to the Motilones. Yes, there have been moments when I wished I had never introduced them to anything from the Western world so that they could retain their sincerity and innocence. I have thought I should have a shotgun to shoot any outsider that comes into the jungle. But the Motilones themselves are wiser than this. They understand that violence engenders violence. And they also see that the outside world was and is encroaching on their lives whether they choose to engage it or not.

The Motilones do not need a protector, as many missionaries would have tried to be for them. Missionaries have attempted to protect the indigenous peoples of Africa, and after a hundred years they still do not have the ability to fend for themselves. The Motilones did not need someone to introduce them to a white man's God, a blond-haired, blue-eyed Jesus, or someone who would teach them how to dress in Western styles and sing "What a Friend We Have in Jesus."

The purpose of entering the mission field is to share the redemptive work of Christ. It starts when the Holy Spirit works in the heart of the person who is going to share the gospel. Then the compassion for the people should help that person share His message in a way that does not strip the people of their autonomy and self-sufficiency and turn them into beggars who depend on benevolent organizations to survive. Many people hear the word *missionary* and equate the term with someone who is trying to destroy native culture, but that is the last thing I want to do.

I have never tried to commercialize Christ. I haven't tried to bribe the Motilones with material rewards for becoming Christian. I haven't even tried to influence them by telling them that medicine comes from God, when in fact it is produced by a pharmaceutical house, or that the schools are a gift from God, when they have been built by gifts from people.

I have learned much from my days in the jungle. I have shared the gospel with the Motilones, and they have shared the practicality of the gospel with me.

What I have tried to do is give the Motilones tools so that they can forge their own future and help them discover that Jesus is not a God who has come to take away their traditions and culture, but a Savior who walked and still walks with them on the trail of life. He is a redeemer who will be with them as they journey beyond the horizon.

Juancho Huamanae, now a doctor in the jungle, was once a medical student at Bucaramanga's Industrial University of Santander (UIS). When a professor there challenged him, saying that I was forcing a white man's religion on him and his people, he responded with these words:

> Bruce's Christian witness has not clashed with our traditional values; quite to the contrary, we discovered Christ incarnate in our midst, who by God's grace, is our redeemer through His death and resurrection. We cherish Christian scriptures in our language, which do not diminish the legitimacy of our verbal traditions or inheritance. In Scripture we find the expectation our elders strove for—reconciliation with our Creator.

What, then, do I see for the future? Only God knows for certain, but I do have ideas on what I hope and believe may take place.

For the mission field, my wish is that subsequent generations will be less interested in constructing fences and more dedicated to building relationships with the people they wish to serve. And I have seen evidence that more missionary programs are moving in this direction. Many are beginning to realize that our ways are not superior to those of native peoples because we have accumulated wealth or things. Rather than constructing a compound filled with beautiful homes and high walls that are off limits to the Indians, they are living among the native people, showing respect for their culture and values. Of course, there may be conflicts between the will of God and the lifestyles of native people. But I believe that the love of Christ and the influence of the Holy Spirit will resolve these differences in the hearts of new believers.

For Colombia, my adopted country, the future is difficult to predict. The region is plagued by many complex problems. The government is still beset by corruption. The guerrilla movement, financed in part by the drug trade and opposed by the government and paramilitary forces, continues to incite violence. The Colombian drug cartels, which cultivate more coca than anyone in the world and supply nearly 80 percent of the world's cocaine,[2] remain a powerful and violent influence. Tensions with the neighboring countries to the east and south, Venezuela and Ecuador, are high. One reason is Colombian President Uribe's friendly stance toward the United States; Venezuelan President Hugo Chavez is an outspoken critic of the current U.S. administration.

My prayer for Colombia and its neighbors is that God will use His servants to bridge the gaps between these opposing forces, bringing about understanding and a lasting peace. It is a monumental task, but there are no limits to what God can do. Who would have believed that hundreds of guerrillas would turn over their lives to Christ after my abduction or that more than one thousand would lay down their arms in a bid for peace in 2004? At the request of President Chavez, I sent him a report on our cooperatives and other programs, and he recently applied some of the same principles to the indigenous populations in Venezuela. Perhaps it is a small first step.

For the five thousand Motilones living among the four hundred thousand members of indigenous tribes in northeastern Colombia, I would like to see a continued commitment to the five-point community development plan we began so many years ago. I hope that the twenty-three health centers now operating, attended by more than twenty-five nurses and eight physicians graduated from Colombian universities through our scholarships, will expand in equipment and expertise. I hope that the twenty-eight agricultural centers, many of them managed by Motilone agronomy graduates from city universities, will continue to produce a host of healthy food products for the Indian communities.

What I have tried to do is give the
Motilones tools so that they can forge their
own future and help them discover that
Jesus is not a God who has come
to take away their traditions and culture,
but a Savior who walked and still walks
with them on the trail of life.

Over the years we have organized more than one hundred twenty jungle schools for various indigenous people groups in eighteen languages and prepared bilingual teachers for the instruction of students. My wish is that these schools will grow in number and capability, continuing to draw the Motilones, other indigenous peoples, and Spanish-speaking Colombians together in an atmosphere of mutual respect. In the past, we have also sponsored as many as forty-eight university students at a time in the cities. Since I am in debt due to my previous scholarship support, however, I have had to cut off my personal financial support of this program. The cooperative directors, still trying to recover from guerrilla takeovers of several of the co-ops, also recently voted against funding new education scholarships. Today, less than twenty students are currently attending Colombian universities. My prayer is that the Motilones will find the means to renew this vital effort.

The attorneys who have already graduated from Colombian law schools are working hard to secure legal protections for traditional Indian territories. Today, perhaps 55 percent of the land entrusted over the centuries to the Motilones is now recognized legally as theirs. My prayer is that these lands will stay protected, both legally and in practice, and that the Indians will be able to legally secure even more of their traditional territory.

Finally, I hope to see the cooperatives, which have struggled in recent years because of the guerrilla intrusions, achieve stability and flourish as in the past, providing the Motilones with an economic system that is both profitable and equitable.

More than any of these steps, however, I pray that my brothers and sisters in the jungle will continue to walk in the footsteps of Saymaydodji-ibateradacura, their leader. Roughly nine of every ten Motilones now follow God incarnate. We have translated the New Testament from Greek into two tribal languages and are training native linguists for continuing translations. The Motilones remain ambassadors for Christ among the neighboring tribes and to the outside world. They have developed a maturity in their faith that would be the envy of nearly any congregation today. I have every confidence that this will continue long after I am gone.

I recently had a conversation about the changes the Motilones have seen in the last forty years and what it has meant to their faith with Ocdabidayna, one of Bobby's closest friends and the first Motilone to be baptized. This is what he said to me:

Besides graduating physicians, forest rangers, pedagogics, lawyers, nurses, bookkeepers (and the like) from Colombian universities, we have the secrets of the piping turkey in the jungle canopy, the mystery of the cave's echo, and the spirit of the fish guide entrusted to us by our tribal elders. On the trail of life's experience, we sing a new song. We step in Jesus' tracks. He is our redeemer!

We have His words now written in our language—the Barí New Testament. It is about His life. And we live in harmony with the jungle creations because of His grace, just as He lives within us.

Ocdabidayna has never seen a road or car, but he is at home in his environment. He can still outrun a deer and outsmart a band of monkeys. He is in training to be a guardian of the histories and legends of the Motilones. Ocdabidayna can recount almost flawlessly more than twenty-four continuous hours of memorized material.

He frequently uses his gift to sing of the New Testament in epic poetry, to the pleasure and fascination of fellow tribal members. In the evening, they will gather at the longhouse, fires still flickering after a sumptuous dinner of roasted fish or monkey meat, and climb into their hammocks. A gentle breeze may float in from the Rio de Oro nearby. A macaw, disguised somewhere in the lush vegetation all around, may call out. And all are content as they listen once more to the stories and wisdom of Saymaydodji-ibateradacura, their leader and hope. The message is presented in the unique, lyrical style of the Motilones and offered in their own language, but its truth is universal. It is our connection, our common thread in the tapestry that God weaves daily among His people around the world.

For the mission field, my wish is that subsequent generations will be less interested in constructing fences and more dedicated to building relationships with the people they wish to serve.

For myself, Bruce Olson, the future is difficult to discern. For the first time in forty-five years, I sense a freedom from God to explore new possibilities. I recently taught courses on linguistics and enjoyed that opportunity. In earlier years I received offers to teach or to serve with mission organizations in the United States, and more recently I was asked to join the faculty of a school of theology in Norway. These are intriguing options, but to move away permanently from my adopted family in the jungle could leave me with a longing that would be too much to bear.

I also find myself contemplating the idea of forming my own family. For years after the death of Gloria, I told myself that I would never fall in love again. To win a woman's respect and commitment to marry and then lose her was something I did not think I could ever repeat. Even when offered Motilone wives over the years I have always declined, thinking that it wouldn't be right. If I had known then what I know now—that I would stay among the Motilones for forty-five years—I wonder if I would have been more open to the idea of the love and companionship of a Motilone wife. The idea of sharing my life with someone, and perhaps even children, has occupied my thoughts more in recent years than it did when I was younger. Perhaps it is too late; perhaps not. It is a matter for prayer.

Of course, the day is surely approaching when God will decide that His need for me on this planet has come to an end. When that time arrives, I will accept it without remorse. I will miss so many loved ones, but I look forward with great anticipation to joining Jesus. That will be a moment to celebrate!

One of my good friends, Araybachira, has told me more than once, "Yado, wherever you die, I will recover your body and take you back to the jungle. Then we will wrap you in a hammock, lift you into the jungle canopy, and offer you to the vultures so that you can travel beyond the horizon as one of us."

I too have tried to walk in the footsteps
of Saymaydodji-ibateradacura on the
trail of life's experience. And in doing so,
I have found the peace that
passes all understanding.

I deeply appreciate those words. Such matters are in God's hands, but I know it would mean much to my brothers and sisters in the jungle if it became so. And I can think of no better conclusion to my earthly existence, nor a better beginning to my new life in eternity.

No matter what happens in the years ahead, I trust that I will be content. More times than I can count, God has given me protection and comfort when I have sought His will and followed His plan. I too have tried to walk in the footsteps of Saymaydodji-ibateradacura on the trail of life's experience. And in doing so, I have found the peace that passes all understanding.

I am especially grateful today to have been allowed into a family of people known as the Motilones. I love them dearly. Perhaps my life with them and their transition from a belligerent, Stone Age tribe into sophisticated and willing servants of Christ *is* a miracle. If so, it is a miracle made by God, and one I will cherish until that day I journey beyond the horizon to rest at last with Him.

Postscript

By James Lund

B ruce Olson is one of the most remarkable individuals I have ever met. Through a simple yet profound commitment made as a teenager—to follow the will of God, wherever it may lead—he has transformed a native people, stood firm in the face of death, and taken the gospel where no one thought possible. The tribal communities that make up the Motilones are now equipped, spiritually and practically, to forge their own future. It would not have been possible without the efforts of a man they originally called "Bruchko." One wonders if the Motilones would even exist today if not for his intervention.

Bruce is too humble to take much credit for these achievements. He rightfully points out that it is God who orchestrates the miracles in our lives and that the glory always belongs to Him. But many have commented over the years on the impact of one man's willingness to be used. One of these commentators is James Thomas Walz, who in 2000 published his study on Bruce and the concept of sacrificial leadership in a doctoral dissertation presented at Regent University. He concluded, in part, with these words:

> The life of Bruce Olson provides us with an example of individual leadership, duty, and responsibility that is as old as humankind itself and mandated in biblical scripture. Although Olson's life is in a setting that is unlike most Western cultural settings, there are some universal truths that must be examined in regard to how individual Christians and the New Testament Church, as a whole, is to conduct itself and the priorities it sets. Bruce Olson's approach to life seems closer to the commission that is given to all Christians, which is exemplified in Romans 12:1: "Present your bodies a living sacrifice, holy, acceptable to God, which is your reasonable service. And do not be conformed to this world, but be transformed by the renewing of your mind, that you may prove what is that good and acceptable and perfect will of God."
>
> Olson has literally offered his life to God as a sacrifice to go and do whatever he believes God is asking of him. He made this commitment very early in life and has remained consistent to his promise. This sacrifice is truly one that few "ordinary" people may ever have the privilege of experiencing. To this day, Olson is ready to make the supreme sacrifice, if needed, to fulfill God's calling for him and the people of Colombia and Venezuela. Many people in our society can rightfully be called "Servant

Leaders," but I suspect that there are only a few who would go to the extent of service that Olson has, risking his own life on a daily basis to become the epitome of what I call a "Sacrificial Leader."[1]

According to Robert Walker, editor emeritus of *Charisma and Christian Life* magazine, *Bruchko,* the book that tells the story of Bruce's work among the Motilones up to the point of Bobby's death, has been published in eighteen languages. As of November 2005, the English version has been reprinted forty-three times in order to keep up with the demand over the years. It has also been reported to the publisher that *Bruchko* has become required reading for several missions training programs.

In the foreword of *Bruchko,* Walker says of Bruce, "He speaks fifteen languages. His findings have appeared in prestigious linguistic journals. He has pioneered in computer translation of tribal languages. As a close personal friend of four presidents of Colombia, he has spoken before the United Nations and the Organization of American States and received many honors for his contributions to the medical and social well-being of South American Indians."

In 1966, the *St. Paul Pioneer Press* featured a story on Bruce, written by Leslie H. Stobbe of the *Chicago Tribune.* In the article, Stobbe said of Bruce, "He has supporters in key positions throughout the governments and in the business communities of Colombia and Venezuela. And when he returned to America in 1965, he received invitations to speak at Northwestern, Princeton, and Harvard universities."

Stobbe described Bruce as "an unusual combination of Christian mystic, anthropologist, linguist, missionary, and one-man Peace Corps. Yet he has remained humble and determined to spread Christianity where no one else has dared to go."[2]

Those who have the privilege of meeting Bruce today would probably agree that not much has changed about him over the past forty years. He speaks self-effacingly about his contributions to the Motilones, and his humility seems to blind him from the fact that people the world over have been inspired by his sacrificial life. Indeed, it is the opinion of only one people group that matters to him: his beloved Motilones.

It is most fitting, therefore, for the Motilones themselves to have the last word on Bruce. Below is their dedication to him in the Motilone-authored publication *Ichidji ya ababi.* It is a small sign of the esteem and love they clearly hold for their dear friend and brother in Christ:

To Yado, Bruce Olson, our father, who has permitted us to watch a new horizon and ring a new dawn, he took us by the hands and taught us that many paths exist in order to know the truth. In the soul, our affection, respect, and admiration will last alongside the wind, the water, and the infinite greenery of the Catatumbo.[3]

Appendix A

A Word to Future Missionaries

I am often asked if I would advise today's young people to do as I did and purchase a one-way ticket to the mission field with little money or support. My answer is a resounding *No!* Young people need to do what God is telling *them* to do, not what God told *me* to do.

These are the principles that were part of my decision to go to South America, which I feel are the same principles that will help any person making a decision to follow the path to which God is leading them.

- Reading the Scriptures
- Applying the Scriptures
- Cultivating a growing relationship with Christ
- Being adopted into the family of God through a local church
- Listening to spiritual leaders
- Hearing the voice of the Holy Spirit
- Having the Spirit's voice confirmed through other Christians and spiritual leaders
- Bearing witness in your own heart of what is being said and confirming the process with those in spiritual leadership over you

As a young Christian, I found spiritual growth through the disciplines of the church. At fourteen, I began to feel an inner nudge to share God's love and life with those who had never known Him. In spite of discouragement from many around me, I sensed a wonderful reassurance that, with God by my side, I could do anything. I learned the difference between plunging ahead in your own power and waiting for His guidance. The Lord knew how inadequate I was, and His preparation came in a series of remarkable incidents that are recorded both in this book and in *Bruchko*.

But it seems to me that today's young people have changing values. They are facing an emotional crisis. They are more sophisticated, yet they are too dependent on others and find it hard to hear and follow the voice of the Spirit.

When I went to South America, I didn't have the fellowship of others upon whom I could depend. I had only the voice of God leading me on the path I was to take.

I believe people grow spiritually by reading, knowing, and hearing God's Word, and by keeping what they receive of God in their hearts. When the Lord began to show me different ways of conducting mission work while I was still in my teens, I kept those things in my heart. My approach was very different from the way mission work was done at that time, but I knew it was God's path for me.

I knew that the Motilones did not have to become Westernized in order to become Christians. They met Jesus right where they live—in the jungle. They know the reality of His redemption on the cross, because He was born among "us" and walked the trails of life's experiences. Jesus became a Motilone.

How did this happen? Because my focus was on respecting and being willing to preserve the culture of the people I was trying to reach for Christ. I was willing to help them find solutions to the challenges they faced within their own culture rather than assuming they needed to adopt my culture and values.

Mission organizations often like to say they are sending missionaries to *serve*. While it is noble to serve others, it is much more important to give them the tools they need to forge their own future. I demonstrated this principle when, instead of challenging the authority of the traditional Indian leaders—the medicine men and women and the chieftains of the various tribes—I earned their trust and allowed them to introduce medical and agricultural advances to the rest of their people. The old maxim is true: if you *give* a man a fish, you feed him for one day; if you *teach* a man to fish, you feed him for a lifetime.

We are often taught that everything is black and white, that everything is either right or wrong. But I have come to feel differently. While the Bible does provide absolutes for us to live by, I think that many things are gray, meaning that the Bible doesn't really address them as right or wrong. But threaded throughout that gray there is a path of white that is the right way to go, based on God's will for each individual. It is up to each one of us to hear and follow God's voice. It will shine like a flashlight that evaporates the gray, like sunlight evaporates a morning fog, and shows us the black and white path for each one of our lives.

As the psalmist said, "Your word is a lamp to my feet and a light for my path" (Ps. 119:105). God will show you each step you are to take and give you the vision for the tasks He is calling you to undertake. Remember, a task without a vision makes a drudgery; a vision without a task makes a visionary; a task and a vision make a missionary.

May your heart be encouraged as you seek God and ask Him what it is that He would have you to do.

Badidina (greetings in Barí), *abrazos* (with a hug, in Spanish), and warmest Christian affection,

—BRUCE OLSON

Appendix B

Chronology of Bruce Olson and the Motilones

November 10, 1941	Bruce is born in Minnesota
1955–1956	Bruce accepts Christ at age fourteen, starts attending a nondenominational church
1958	Bruce hears a missionary from New Guinea speak and senses a call to the mission field
Early 1961	Bruce leaves college and arrives in Venezuela at age nineteen; Bruce travels with Dr. Christian and stays three months with Indians on the Mavaca River in the Orinoco region; Bruce is infected with Chagas' disease
Early 1962	Bruce makes his way to the Yuko Indians
July 1962	Bruce is ambushed by Motilones and held captive for one month
September 1962	Bruce returns to Motilones after escaping to Bogotá, Colombia
Early 1963	Bruce and Bobaríshora (Bobby) become pact brothers
Early to mid-1960s	Arabadoyca is first Motilone to venture into the outside world—Cúcuta; meets President Guillermo Valencia
Early to mid-1960s	Motilone medicine woman begins using modern medicine
Early to mid-1960s	Jorge Kaymiyokba is orphaned, attends boarding school, and becomes first Motilone to study outside of the jungle
1963	Bruce begins constructing first Motilone health clinic
1965	Bruce meets Gloria
1966	First bilingual school in the jungle is established
Late 1966	Bobby accepts Christ; soon after, Bobby and Atacadara are married; Bruce begins translating New Testament into Barí language
December 1966	Bobby accompanies Bruce and becomes the first Motilone to travel to the United States; he meets Bruce's parents and speaks at the United Nations
1967	Arabadoyca and the Motilones share the gospel with the Yukos

Late 1960s	First successful co-ops established; Motilones feed Don Jorge's family; Bobby adopts Odo; Samuel Greenberg studies the Motilones
1968	Bruce purchases two abandoned houses, Axdobaringcayra and Buiyocbacbaringcayra, from an oil company
1969	Bobby's daughter, Cuadudura, is born
1970	Bruce is reunited with Gloria in Bogotá, they become engaged; Gloria dies in car crash
1971	Two health centers have been established and are staffed by Motilones who have been trained in basic health care practices; two bilingual schools for the Motilones are now in operation; Bruce becomes Colombian citizen
August 4, 1972	Bobby is murdered by land settlers; Odo's speech inspires the tribe to carry on Bobby's vision for their people
December 1972	Jorge Kaymiyokba translates Odo's speech at Colombia's Third Congress on Community Development in Cúcuta; Jorge Kaymiyokba receives Medallion of Excellence from President Misael Pastrana
March 1974	President Misael Pastrana signs legislation granting Motilones 205,000 acres, equal to 320 square miles, as their territory
Summer 1974	Tornado rips through health care center treating Motilones with tuberculosis
1974	Four bilinguals schools have been established in the jungle, three of them serving Motilones *and* colonists; eight health centers now exist, treating colonists as well as Motilones
Mid-1970s	Fred and his family visit the Motilones; Fred builds a door
Mid-1970s	Bruce sells textiles to shop owner in Texas to help fund Motilone scholarships
1976–1977	Andres Küng visits Bruce and writes his book
1977	Bruce speaks at his father's retirement banquet in Minnesota
Fall 1978	Bruce and his father are reconciled
1979	Jorge Kaymiyokba is named first president of newly formed Motilone-Barí Community of Colombia Association; Waysersera is named vice president
March 1979	Bruce's father, Marcus Olson, dies; Bruce's mother, Inga Olson, dies several years later

Fall 1979	Bruce is offered positions with a Methodist mission organization and a Norwegian school of theology, turns both down to stay with the Motilones
1983	Jorge Kaymiyokba's eight-year-old son, Chidisayra, dies; Kaymiyokba continues to serve his people and is elected director of the Fraternity of Eastern Colombian Tribal Peoples
1984	Fidel Waysersera, first Motilone to attend a Western university, is appointed secretary of Indian affairs
1985	Fidel Waysersera and Roberto Dacsarara are the first Motilones to graduate from national universities
November 13, 1985	Volcanic eruption of Nevado del Ruiz kills 27,000; Motilone doctors and nurses help treat the wounded
1986	Colombian government recognizes the Motilone-Barí Cooperative and the AsocBarí Trading Post as legally registered cooperatives
1986	There are now seven bilingual schools in the jungle with more than 450 students, including Motilones, colonists, and other Indian tribes; more than fifty Motilones have graduated from the jungle schools and gone on to attend high school or apprenticeship programs in the city
August 1986	President Belasario Bentancur invites Bruce and four Motilones—Jorge Kaymiyokba, Roberto Dacsarara, Fidel Waysersera, and Daniel Adjibacbayra—to attend the Third Congress of Frontier Policies in Cúcuta
Late 1980s	Guerrilla forces begin to confront Motilones
Late 1987	The Book of James is translated by Bruce and Jorge Kaymiyokba; Bruce survives poisonous bushmaster snake bite
Early 1988	Colombia's minister of national defense warns Bruce that he is a military target
October 24, 1988	Bruce is abducted by the ELN on the Rio de Oro, spends four months chained to a tree in the jungle
Early 1989	Guerrillas release photograph and note from Bruce, letting the Motilones know he is alive; Bruce teaches literacy classes to the guerrillas, becomes camp cook and dentist; 120 guerrillas accept Christ as Savior
Spring 1989	Pérez visits Bruce in captivity; Bruce is moved from camp to camp; military forces bomb guerrillas who are holding Bruce hostage

Summer 1989	Bruce is tortured by guerrillas, receives blood transfusion from Camillo
July 1989	Alejandro announces that Bruce's execution has been scheduled
July 19, 1989	Bruce is released to journalists on the Colombia-Venezuela border
August 1989	Bruce meets with President Barco and recounts his captivity
1990	At Barco's invitation, Bruce participates in the formation of the Colombian Peace Commission; grenade explodes in Bruce's car
1990–1992	Peace talks break down; ELN makes new threats on Bruce's life
1992	Fidel Waysersera and Roberto Dacsarara represent Motilones at United Nations Congress on Environment and Development (Earth Summit) in Rio de Janeiro; Roberto Dacsarara speaks at conference and convinces the Colombian government to grant the Motilones the legal right to their territory
1996	National Agrarian Reform legislation enacted, legally returning most of the lowlands to Motilones, adding to their territory
May 1997	ELN releases 300+ Christian "peacemakers" from their ELN oath
November 1997	Bruce is abducted by the EPL; escapes
Early 1999	Series of earthquakes devastate Central Colombia; Motilones send team of four doctors and twenty nurses to help with relief efforts
1999	Bruce and thirty university students are caught in crossfire between guerrillas and paramilitary forces on the way to Bucaramanga
Late 1999	Another attempt on Bruce's life is made
2001	Julio wins Latin Federation of Journalism's "Best Photograph 2001" award for self portrait titled "A Poor Reflection"
May 11, 2002	Bruce is awarded an honorary doctor of divinity at Regent University by Pat Robertson
2003	Guerrillas seize four Motilone co-ops and delivery truck; the Motilones publish *Ichidji ya ababi: Algo nuestro, así somos los Barí*; twenty-three health centers are in operation, twenty-eight agricultural centers, twenty-eight government-certified jungle schools, graduating more than 400 who have gone on to continue their education in the cities, twenty-two co-ops
November 2004	1,400 guerrillas and drug traffickers turn in their weapons and are granted amnesty from the Colombian government

Appendix C

Notes

Chapter 2
Love... and Loss

1. Andres Küng, *Bruce Olson: Missionary or Colonizer?* (Chappaqua, NY: Christian Herald Books, 1977), 179.

Chapter 4
Menace From Above

1. Ibid., 122.

Chapter 5
Respect

1. Open letter written by Jorge Kaymiyokba, published by *El Espectador*, November 7, 1991

2. Ken Mitchell, *Chicago Tribune*, Church News, January 12, 1974, as originally published in Bruce Olson's newsletter to supporters on January 15, 1987.

3. Dr. Stephen Beckerman, Department of Anthropology, University of New Mexico, as originally published in Bruce Olson's newsletter to supporters in September 1975.

4. Rev. Jean Malam, secretary of information, Sweden, as originally published in Bruce Olson's newsletter to supporters in September 1975.

5. Misael Pastrana, president of Colombia, as originally published in Bruce Olson's newsletter to supporters in September 1975.

6. Dr. Harold W. Turner, Scottish Institute of Missionary Studies, University of Aberdeen, Scotland, as originally published in Bruce Olson's newsletter to supporters in September 1975.

7. Jim Reapsome, *World Pulse*, in Nancy Justice, "Ambassador to the Jungle," *Charisma and Christian Life*, August 2000, accessed via http://www.charismamag.com/a.php?ArticleID=454 (accessed March 27, 2006).

8. Küng, *Bruce Olson: Missionary or Colonizer?*, 147.

9. Ibid., 99, italics added.

10. Ibid., 99–100.

11. Ibid., 174

Chapter 10
Increasing Danger

1. Rodney Bobiwash, "Director of Forum for Global Exchange to Visit Colombia," Center for World Indigenous Studies, Olympia, Washington, July 31, 2001, http://www.cwis.org/260fge/minga.html (accessed on January 27, 2006).

2. Raphael Perl, "Drug Control: International Policy and Approaches," CRS Issue Brief for Congress, May 13, 2004, page 1, http://fpc.state.gov/documents/organization/33744.pdf (accessed on February 2, 2006).

Chapter 13
Immature Brothers

1. Maria Cristina Caballero, "A Norwegian Motilone Cries Out for Freedom," *El Tiempo* (Bogotá), June 11, 1989, translation of the Special Sunday edition.

2. Open letter written in the name of the Motilone-Barí Council of Colombia, published by *El Tiempo* (Bogotá), April 25, 1989.

3. Susan Williams, "Bruce Olson's Nine-Month Colombian Captivity," *Charisma and Christian Life*, December 1989, 76.

Chapter 16
Transition to the Twenty-first Century

1. *Ichidji ya ababi: Algo nuestro, así somos los Barí* [All of Us: Something About Who We Are, the Barí] (Tibú, Norte de Santander, Colombia: Editorial AsocBarí, 2003).

Chapter 17
Content With the Future

1. Küng, *Bruce Olson: Missionary or Colonizer?*, 188.

2. "Quick Guide: The Colombian Conflict," BBC NEWS, 2004, news.bbc.co.uk/1/shared/spl/hi/pop_ups/quick_guides/05/americas_the_colombian_conflict/html/1.stm (accessed February 17, 2006).

Postscript

1. James Thomas Walz, "Laying the Groundwork for Sacrificial Leadership: An Interpretive Biographical Study of the Life of Bruce Olson, Missionary and Leader to the Indigenous Tribes of Colombia and Venezuela" (doctoral dissertation, Regent University, 2000).

2. Leslie H. Stobbe, "Arrows into Plowshares: St. Paulite 'Tames' Fierce Jungle Tribe," *St. Paul Pioneer Press*, July 24, 1966, 15.

3. *Ichidji ya ababi: Algo nuestro, así somos los Barí* [All of Us: Something About Who We Are, the Barí] (Tibú, Norte de Santander, Colombia: Editorial AsocBarí, 2003).

Other resources used but not cited:

Bruce Olson, *Bruchko* (Lake Mary, FL: Charisma House, 1995).

Bruce Olson, Newsletters on missionary work, 1970–2005.

Robert Walker, "Jungle Experiment," *Christian Life* 43, June 1981.

You can be a part of Bruce Olson's ministry by contributing to his work through Christian Life Missions. As Bruce senses his time among the Motilones drawing to a close, he is preparing to write a book on missiology detailing the lessons he learned in the South American jungle. Your tax-deductible contribution will help Bruce's ongoing work. Please make your check payable to Christian Life Missions and indicate that it is for Bruce Olson's work. You can contact Christian Life Missions at:

Christian Life Missions
Department BR-06
P. O. Box 952248
Lake Mary, FL 32795-2248
Web site: http://www.christianlifemissions.org
Phone: (407) 333-0600

BETTER THAN FICTION...

Bruchko and the Motilone Miracle has been a remarkable read...full of adventure, tragedy, faith, and love. It has shown how, despite incredible dangers and obstacles, one humble man and a nation of primitive, violent Indians—by joining together in simple obedience—can be transformed forever by the sovereign will of God.

MORE THAN 200,000 COPIES SOLD!

BRUCE OLSON

BRUCHKO

The astonishing true story of a 19-year-old American, his capture by the Motilone Indians and his adventures in Christianizing the Stone Age tribe

1-59185-993-X / $14.99

BP6803

DON'T MISS THE BEGINNING YEARS (1961–1974) IN THE LIFE OF THIS ADVENTUROUS MISSIONARY IN *BRUCHKO*.

Bruchko explains what happens when a nineteen-year-old boy leaves home and heads into the jungles to evangelize a murderous tribe of South American Indians. For Bruce Olson it meant capture, disease, terror, loneliness, and torture. But what he discovered by trial and error has revolutionized the world of missions.